First, *Best,*
or *Different*

First, *Best*, or *Different*

What Every Entrepreneur Needs to Know About Niche Marketing

BY JOHN BRADLEY JACKSON

First published by Dog Ear Publishing
4010 W. 86th Street, Ste H
Indianapolis, IN 46268
www.dogearpublishing.net

ISBN: 978-159858-291-8
Library of Congress Control Number: 2007921630

This book is printed on acid-free paper.

Printed in the United States of America

This book is dedicated to all the entrepreneurs
who had the courage, spirit, vision, and tenacity
to create new enterprises, but who may have lacked
the patience to study the inherent risks in creating new
businesses, or who may have just ignored the bleak facts.

"There's a difference between knowing the Path
and walking the Path."

From the movie "The Matrix"
by Larry and Andy Wachowski (1999)

Reviews

"FIRST, BEST, OR DIFFERENT is one of those exceptional books that changes the way you think about marketing and entrepreneurs. The book demystifies marketing and challenges the reader to focus on the customer, which is what it is all about. Author John Bradley Jackson pulls this off in a thought provoking, yet easy to read style. I highly recommend this book."

Manny Fernandez, Chairman Emeritus, Gartner Inc.

"Are you an entrepreneur struggling with marketing? FIRST, BEST, OR DIFFERENT will take years off your ad hoc approach and shorten your sales cycle. John Bradley Jackson goes to the heart of the matter, bringing insider information and secrets to small businesses. In my 25 years of consulting, this is the most valuable book I've read on effective marketing techniques. Read it 'first' before your competitors!"

Jim Kelton, President, Altius Information Technologies Inc.

"As an owner of a small business, Jackson's message about selling with integrity and trust really hit home with me. Successful niche marketing clearly requires a candid dialog between the customer and the entrepreneur. As the book says, it is all about the customer and not me."

Bruce Welch, President, Stellar Engineering Inc.

"If there ever was such a thing as marketing cookbook for entrepreneurs, John Bradley Jackson's FIRST, BEST, OR DIFFERENT is it. This book is filled with proven recipes for marketers who want to get their companies to the top of the heap and not break the bank in the process!"

Don Collier, President, Prolytix Corporation

"I have found this to be a very logical, well reasoned and balanced book that mixes the practical, tactical and more intuitive elements of managing a business to make money. The author dispels outdated notions of sales and marketing strategies and challenges readers to carefully know their customers, their businesses and most importantly, themselves. This book is a resource that can be returned to time and time again for new initiatives, growth planning, or management audits. I highly recommend it."

Robert Nolan, Principal and Co-founder, NanoMarkets, LC

"FIRST, BEST, OR DIFFERENT should be required reading in any business school. The division of the book into small segments with an interesting and appropriate quote at the beginning of each segment makes for fast paced reading. First-time entrepreneurs should use the book as a road map to success and long-time entrepreneurs should use it as a periodic review of their operation. I have been a small entrepreneur for over 40 years and after reading the first pages, I noted that I should start sending thank you notes with our invoices and start using focus groups for our new ideas. John Bradley Jackson's "first" book is "different" and is "best" for small entrepreneurs."

Duane Gomer, Owner, Duane Gomer Incorporated

"Successful organizations consistently apply the art and science of marketing to drive revenue, win market share and produce profit. Jackson's book, FIRST, BEST, OR DIFFERENT, demystifies many commonly misunderstood concepts of marketing and introduces the reader to useful and best practices of skilled marketers. Read it, apply it, and prosper!"

Frank Sammann, Member, Board of Directors, Biz360 Incorporated

"If you are a fast-paced entrepreneur running at top speed with hopes of increasing your sales, this is a must read. Jackson offers the tools you need for success in a niche market including clear, crisp insight and real-world examples to keep you on the right path. Being different is what counts."

Ken Townsend, Sales Manager, WestAmerica Graphics

Preface

Successful entrepreneurs have great courage along with a vision of what can be done. Yet, my consulting work with entrepreneurs along with my own experience in niche market environments has taught me about the greater significance that a well-thought-out and properly executed marketing plan has on the success of a venture. In practice, most entrepreneurs have had precious little marketing training; instead, they have learned on the job. While some may have succeeded, many struggled with the art of niche marketing and were overwhelmed by the choices offered in the marketing mix: pricing, promotion, advertising, publicity, channels of distribution, and public relations (to name a few).

Unfortunately, too many entrepreneurs race forward without defining their target market or taking the time to truly understand the customers' needs and problems. In a desperate attempt to create cash flow, they run from one customer to another, offering a solution, which is often off the mark. Statistically, most businesses fail due to the absence of a concrete marketing strategy and to a lack of capital. If they had only slowed down long enough to create a substantive marketing plan, they might have avoided frustration and, possibly, failure.

In response to the entrepreneur's need for help in understanding these marketing choices, this book is about marketing with a sense of purpose and vision, understanding customer needs, defining the market, crafting a needs-based solution, creating intimacy and trust with the customer, and doing it right the first time. I have written the book to demystify the sometimes overly complex nomenclature of marketing by writing it in plain English, by using easy-to-read short chapters, and by offering numerous ideas on how to market better and sell more. Absent from the book is any tedious debate on what the various marketing terms mean; instead, you will find short definitions and practical insight. All these suggestions come from successful entrepreneurs that I have known and from my own personal experience.

For the record, I struggled with the word "entrepreneur" which is French for someone who creates or operates a business, is personally accountable for the success or failure of the business, and contends with risk. A common usage today of the word "entrepreneur" is someone who has vision or is innovative, whether in a small or a large organization. Small businesses may or may not be innovative, but they certainly contend with risk. You will note that I sometimes use "entrepreneur" and "small business" interchangeably, which is not technically correct. I defend myself by aligning with the others in the business press who also confuse the terms.

Acknowledgments

I am forever thankful for the support from Jerry Banks, Brad Barrett, Jeff Black, Shelly Berggren, Greg Bertrand, Mike Bry, Jose Calero, Sean Cantelon, Jim Carr, Reid Carter, Curtis Chan, Elaine Chu, Don Collier, Steve Cooper, Ken Crooks, Kevin Eikenberry, Sally Donovan, Guy Dufresne, Bill Erickson, Roger Essam, Sean Fares, Manny Fernandez, Steve Forell, Don Gage, Mike Gancar, Duane Gomer, Neil Harle, Tom Hartley, Russ Hearl, Alfred Herzing, Bob Hooven, John Ishimaru, Bob Jackovich, Sheri Jackson, Kelly Johnson, Greg Jordan, Charles Keane, Chris Kelley, Jim Kelton, Garrett Kop, Bob Kreisberg, Randy Likas, Liz Levy, Curtis Ludlow, Dana Luvera, Dennis Lyftogt, David Lynn, Paul Magargee, Alan Mannason, Pat Marshment, Craig McLaughlin, Lynn Melton, Nichole Mirabile, Bonni Montevecchi, Mike Murphy, Mike Murray, Alison Nasisi, Greg Nelson, Robert Nolan, Elo Okpei, Jan Oncel, Paul Oronoz, Sangita Patel, Nathalie Pignatiello, Dave Primac, Stu Quinn, Jerry Ramos, Doug Rogers, John Regan, John Rosica, Jennifer Rudd-O'Neil, Doug Rugg, Mike Sadeghpour, Teresa Saldivar, Barbara Samara, Frank Sammann, Ron Schott, Gary Schultz, Earl Skakel, Michelle Smith, Bill Smyth, Doug Sproal, Sheridan Tatsuno, Oli Thordarson, Ken Townsend, Tom Underhill, Greg Wallace, Tim Walworth, Bruce Welch, Bruce Wells, Dave Wheeler, and Paul Wisdom.

I am also thankful for the support of my brothers and sisters, Craig, Clark, Bruce, Marlys, Gail, Jess, and Ross along with their spouses and children. All were very helpful in the choice of the book title, which was decided, in large part at the family barbeque on the Fourth of July 2006.

Additionally, I want to thank all my students at the Center for Entrepreneurship at California State University, Fullerton, who braved my class and challenged me to write this book. Entrepreneurs themselves, the students were a constant inspiration to write this book so that we could better help our entrepreneur clients. Frankly, we learned a lot from each other, and I may have learned the most from them. Thanks also to my in-class coaches whose time-tested experience as entrepreneurs and marketers helped guide my students and me. My appreciation also goes out to our consulting clients who welcomed the students into their businesses and gave us the opportunity to better understand the marketing challenges with new ventures.

I am deeply appreciative of the support from my marketing mentors, Dr. Irene Lange and Dr. Michael Ames at California State University, Fullerton; both inspired me to make this book a reality.

Special thanks to Judy Herrick who helped me clean up my grammar and who also taught me some special lessons about the search for meaning, purpose, spirituality, and personal significance.

Most of all, I must thank my lovely supportive wife Janet and my beautiful children Beth, Tom, and Valla.

Table of Contents

1. First, Best, or Different

"Entrepreneurs are simply those who understand that there
is little difference between obstacle and opportunity
and are able to turn both to their advantage."

Niccolo Machiavelli (1469–1527) Italian writer and statesman

The entrepreneur who finds a customer segment that has been under-served or overlooked can earn extraordinary rewards. Niche marketing requires that you focus on customers who cannot get what they want or need from their existing providers. For various reasons, mainstream firms will often innocently overlook or deliberately pass over customers with special needs; instead, they will choose to market to the larger, more homo-geneous customer groups. These underserved or overlooked segments can be very fertile ground for the entrepreneur to exploit, since they need a provider who truly understands their requirements.

By focusing on these customer segments the entrepreneur can differ-entiate their offerings from that of the competition while creating loyal cus-tomers which will be a source of referrals. Additionally, the entrepreneur may be rewarded with higher margins and longer product life cycles. Every entrepreneur needs to know that to be successful in niche marketing you need to be first, best, or different.

Being first can be enough in some markets to capture a great reward. A business can differentiate itself by being the first to solve the customers' needs; these customers and their unique needs may have been passed over by other firms. Unfortunately, it is hard to defend that position long term, presuming the market is big enough for more than one competitor. Some-times being first creates a loud "buzz", a public relations euphoria associ-ated with the new solution. You may have witnessed this buzz in the software industry when innovative products hit the market. The product is the "new thing" and everybody seems to want it, at least until something faster or better comes along. When a second player enters the market with a better product, and this is often the case, the buzz for the first product goes silent, making the first firm a "one-hit wonder". Thus, being first is seldom sustainable in the long term.

Being the best may be the optimum state for the entrepreneur. This implies that the solution provides exactly what the customers need today; most often this fit is derived from an intimate understanding of the cus-tomers' wants and needs while offering a perfect or best solution. The customers value the solution above all others and may tolerate paying a higher price. Because of their loyalty, they may even be a source of referrals for your firm which helps create market-share dominance. The challenge in this case is how to stay on top. If the market is big enough, other firms will eventually want a piece of this market. If the competitors have sufficient capital and the barriers to entry are low, the first entrepreneur may struggle to defend its best position. Being best is easier when the market niche is very small and your firm is the only significant player. This positioning may be the "nirvana" of niche marketing, but I don't know of many of them.

This leaves being different as the remaining option for most entrepreneurs. In this environment, the solution offered is unique enough to be a better choice for the customers; an example of this might be the Ferrari. The Ferrari, with its unique styling and high-end performance, is considered different to the point of being exotic and is highly valued by a special segment of automobile buyers. Ferrari has a loyal following, has few real competitors, and commands a very special price for the car's unique attributes.

Alternatively, things can be done differently. My favorite example of doing the same thing differently is Starbucks, where a pedestrian product like a cup of coffee is delivered, packaged, and sold as a lifestyle item. In return, Starbucks commands a premium price and is rewarded with incredible brand equity. We can argue about their product quality, but essentially, they are doing things differently rather than offering something different. Being different or doing things differently tends to be the domain of many successful entrepreneurs.

To be successful, an entrepreneur has to be first to market, has to be the absolute best, or has to be demonstratively different from the competition. While it may be "possible" to be all three (first, best, and different), the challenge for the business is to be sustainable over the long term. Can you name any businesses that are first, best, and different and have withstood the test of time? It is truly a short list and subject to great debate.

Coca-Cola comes to mind as a firm that might be first, best, and different, but some would argue about the firm being first, best, or different. Coca-Cola was actually beat to market by a "coca-wine" which was initially sold as a headache medicine; but Coke was the first mass-marketed soft drink. Pepsi drinkers might argue that Coke is not best by citing the "Pepsi Challenge", which was a blind taste test that showed that cola drinkers had a preference for Pepsi over Coke. Is Coke different? People have voted yes with their dollars with Coca-Cola topping $43 billion in 2005 revenues; remember, "Coke is It." There is no doubt that Coca-Cola has been a sustainable brand; it was founded in 1886 and has been a cultural phenomena. It must be said that Coca-Cola is not exactly a niche player, but it illustrates the point that it is hard to be all three: first, best, and different.

Thus, the choices that remain for the successful entrepreneur tend to favor the creation of a unique offering for a special customer that has not been served well or at all by the other providers; this is the essence of niche marketing. As for which niche market to choose, that is up to you. Making that choice a reality then becomes a matter of designing, implementing and managing your niche market strategy, which we will discuss in much detail in this book; but, before launching this strategy, you must define your purpose.

Your action: Write down a list of your product's features that make it different. These differences can make the basis for your marketing message.

2. Mission and Vision: What is Your Purpose?

"Make your work to be in keeping with your purpose."

Leonardo da Vinci (1452–1519) Scientist, inventor, and artist

You are going to end up somewhere, so why not end up where you want to be? Organizations all have a purpose or a reason for being. Many call it a mission. That mission helps the firm to make good decisions that are consistent with its purpose. With a well written "mission statement" to guide you, the little decisions for your firm become easier, and I think you have a better chance of getting to your desired destination.

A mission statement is a proclamation about why the firm exists and what really matters. It should speak about the firm's values and describe what the business hopes to achieve while describing the nature of the business. A mission statement can provide a compass during times of uncertainty or strife by reminding the employees at the firm about what really matters.

The mission statement should be a few sentences up to a brief paragraph that is simple, clear, and jargon free. No Shakespeare needed here. Thirty words or less should do the trick. It should be memorable, while motivating to the firm's employees. If properly written, the mission statement can be displayed proudly on the company website, brochures, and business cards.

Your mission statement should include some or most of these elements:

- Who is your customer?
- What business are you in?
- What are your products or services?
- What is your geographic domain?
- What is your commitment to ownership?
- How is your firm different from the competition?
- What are the opportunities available for the firm?
- What is your company philosophy?
- What are the firm's core beliefs and values?
- What is the essence of your brand?
- What do things look like when things go well?

A vision statement, while similar to a mission statement, is more of a proclamation of what the firm should be; it is an image of the desired future, almost utopian in its grandeur. Typically, the vision statement is no more than a short sentence. Some say that a vision statement is a description of an ideal and, thus, it will never be achieved. Most vision statements are imaginative and hope to inspire others.

What you need to do: Take a stab at answering the questions above; you have ten minutes.

3. How to Write a Corporate Mission Statement

"Alice came to a fork in the road.
"Which road do I take?" she asked.
"Where do you want to go?" responded the Cheshire cat.
"I don't know," Alice answered.
"Then," said the cat, "it doesn't matter."

Lewis Carroll (1832–1898) Author

Writing the corporate mission statement is a team effort. First, gather a cross-sectional team from your organization; involve all levels from your firm, not just you and not just senior management. A mission statement written by the boss or a few senior managers won't be as good as the one written by a team comprised of people from all levels of the organization. There is incredible power in the wisdom of a diverse team. Additionally, by involving a cross-sectional team, you create evangelists for the final mission statement. The following list describes the basic steps to create a mission statement:

- List your firm's strengths.
- List your firm's unique competencies.
- List your major customers or target markets.
- List your firm's core values.
- List the things the firm is dedicated to such as quality, customer satisfaction, etc.
- Rank each list by importance.
- Combine categories whenever possible.
- Turn the lists into short sentences.
- Rank the sentences by importance.
- Combine the most important sentences into a paragraph.
- Wordsmith the paragraph using real words; beware of fancy jargon or buzz words and try to use no more than 30 words.
- Test the draft paragraph on other team members, customers, and suppliers.
- Revise the paragraph based on the feedback received.
- Post the mission statement everywhere.
- Agree to review this statement once a year to verify its authenticity; better yet, review the mission statement quarterly.

Your mission should now be on full display. Place it on your website, on the back of your business cards, in your wallet, everywhere that you can post it. Post it in your lobby. Some mission statements may be for internal consumption only and may not be appropriate for customers and that's OK. For example, being insanely profitable may be a fine mission for you, but your customers may not find it so.

Final thought: Focus and it will expand. Think big.

4. *Values: What Really Matters Most to You?*

"Always do right. This will gratify some people and astonish the rest."

Mark Twain (1835–1910) Humorist and author

Values are the foundation of the individual. Values are our belief system; they express what is meaningful and important and they are the rules by which we run our lives. Every entrepreneur has a set of values. These values form boundaries on our behavior for our morals and our ethics. These rules help us to make decisions, set goals, and monitor our behavior.

At a business, the firm's values are created in large part by the values of the leadership. These values can be many things such as hard work, commitment to quality, and putting the customer first. The potential list of values is long, but what really matters is what is most important to the entrepreneur and, thus, the firm. Being in touch with these core values is essential to developing and delivering a believable unique value proposition. Quite frankly, doing an inventory of your personal values as an entrepreneur is on the surface simple, but in practice requires a fair amount of soul searching. To do this inventory justice, the entrepreneur needs to reflect and contemplate about things we seldom think about, but unconsciously live by.

A good exercise to unearth your core values would be to look into the future and attend your own funeral. Gathered to say farewell to you are all your family, friends, and colleagues. Your role at the funeral is as the presenter of your own eulogy. It is your last chance to tell your family, friends, and colleagues what your life was really all about. You get the final say on what was important to you as a person; you have no need to hedge your comments, nor do you need to flatter anyone or pretend to be something that you are not. This final good-bye is a way for you to help others with their life choices and help them understand what truly matters. It is your gift to them for a better life.

Does this sound a little heavy for a book on entrepreneurial marketing? Maybe so, but I challenge you to stay in touch with these core values and to fervently defend them, since they are your compass. If you stay true to these values, you will always be successful in your own eyes (your toughest judge).

That said, organizations are challenged on a daily basis to make the right choices; the temptation to compromise these values is great. The challenges could include compromising quality for increased profits, hiding revenue from the government, and accepting orders for products or services that don't fit your mission. Your core values will tell you what is right and what is not. Listen to them.

Therefore, does it pay to be honest, to act with integrity? We know many examples of dishonest and evil people, who became rich, powerful, and famous. The company name Enron conjures up an image of bartered ethics rewarded with immense riches; yet, the consequences of the lies at Enron included shame and prison terms. I think the answer is in the definition of what a "payday" truly is to you. Can you sleep at night knowing that you have broken the law? Will you be respected and admired? How do explain it to your children?

What to do: Write your own eulogy. Share it with a friend or family member.

5. How to Write a Corporate Values Statement

"Those are my principles, and if you don't like them…
well, I have others."

Groucho Marx (1890–1977) Comedian and author

Writing a corporate values statement should be a team effort. Gather a cross-sectional team to avoid the myopia of an "executive only" document and to ensure a feeling of ownership by the whole organization. The mechanics of creating a values statement are similar to that of writing the mission statement. The goal is to have a concise statement or a list of core values for the organization. I frankly prefer a listing of five or six values that speak about what really matters.

A good way to get started would be to review a sample list of values like the one below to get everyone thinking:

- Continuous learning
- Quality
- Customer satisfaction
- Employee job satisfaction
- Integrity
- Dependability
- Accountability
- Respect for the individual
- Honest communication
- Profitability and growth
- Technical superiority
- Best in class or best in breed
- Tradition or history
- Teamwork or team play
- Continuous innovation
- Positive work environment
- Diversity
- Green (environmentally speaking)
- Member of the community
- Trust
- Social responsibility

- Empowerment
- Fun
- Change

Next, have each team member pick five values that are important to them and continue as follows:

- List all these values together and have a discussion about what these values mean.
- Rank these values by importance as it relates to your firm.
- Reduce the values list to the top five or six values.
- Wordsmith the list; I prefer short phrases or just one-word values.
- Test this values list with other team members, suppliers, and customers.
- Adjust the list per the feedback.
- Post the list in the lobby and on the website.

Your action: Create a list of the values that you admire in others.

6. *The 4 Ps and the 4 Cs of Marketing*

"If the circus is coming to town and you paint a sign saying "Circus Coming to the Fairground Saturday," that's advertising. If you put the sign on the back of an elephant and walk it into town, that's promotion. If the elephant walks through the mayor's flowerbed, that's publicity. If you get the mayor to laugh about it, that's public relations. If the town's citizens go the circus, you show them the many entertainment booths, explain how much fun they'll have spending money at the booths, answer their questions and ultimately, they spend a lot at the circus, that's sales."

Unknown

Welcome to Marketing 101. Today's lecture is about the "4 Ps of Marketing." Author E. Jerome McCarthy coined the 4 Ps long ago, and they are marketing gospel today: product, place, price, and promotion.

- Product is the goods, services, or solutions that the provider delivers. This is really the end game for the entrepreneur since it is all about the customer and not the product, but more to come on that later.
- Place is the way or the method that you get your product, service, or solution to the customer. This could be a retail store, a website, or a sales representative.
- Price is the financial exchange for the value that the provider delivers to the customer. The customer deems that the price is right or fair and that your product is worth it. Implicit in this transaction is the fact the customer chose your product instead of the competitor's offering.
- Promotion is the how you get the message to the customer. In the broadest sense, this includes publicity, advertising, and public relations.

The 4 Ps are often called the "marketing mix". For the entrepreneur, the challenge is to adjust this mix of marketing tools to accommodate the changing needs of the competitive environment. For example, pricing might need to be reduced in response to competitive pressures. Alternatively, more advertising might be required to create awareness of the product.

Candidly, the 4 Ps are a bit out of date. The 4 Ps look at marketing from the provider's point of view rather than from the customer perspective. In the new millennium, the customer is in charge and demands to be served their way, when they want it, and where they want. Got it?

Dr. Bob Lauterborn, a professor at the University of North Carolina, gets it. He thinks that we need to toss out the 4 Ps. He contends that there are actually 4 Cs:

- Consumer Wants and Needs—Instead of products first, you need to find what the customer wants and then create the product, service, or solution. This makes too much sense. It is all about the customer, not the solution.
- Cost to Satisfy—Instead of price, think like the customer does. Customers ask the question, "What will it cost me to be satisfied and get what I need". The customer will pay a fair price for a fair deal.
- Convenience to Buy—Instead of place, the more pertinent question is how and where does the customer want to purchase? This question is getting tougher to answer with increasingly segmented consumer markets, the worldwide web, and the global economy.
- Communication—Instead of promotion, which stinks of manipulation or greed, you need to ask the customer questions and listen. Blasting the airwaves with a repetitive advertisement does not work anymore, since the customer is numb from too much advertising, while being more sophisticated than past generations. Customers have access to nearly as much information as providers, much to the consternation of the providers.

The 4 Cs make more sense to me.

Tip: Audit your company's marketing mix. Are you taking full advantage of all the marketing tools available?

7. *The Most Important Choice an Entrepreneur Will Ever Make*

"And now for something completely different."

Monty Python Flying Circus (1969–1974) Comedy troupe

My work with entrepreneurs has shown me that careful positioning of your business in a narrowly defined niche enables success. A laser-like focus for your product or service helps the business say "yes" to what they are good at and say "no" to everything else.

In the book, THE WINNING PERFORMANCE, authors Donald K. Clifford, Jr. and Richard E. Cavanaugh profiled over 6,000 small- to medium-sized firms, which grew at a rate four times that of the Fortune 250. They found that these fast-growing small firms bucked the conventional wisdom of large firms, which focus only sales and profits; instead, they focused on understanding the needs of a specific customer or market segment and marketed only to them.

Too often entrepreneurs take on broad charters or overly complex product lines to generate cash flow. They don't stick to their knitting. They commit themselves to customers that don't fit within their target market, that are low or no margin, and that eat up valuable time. The temptation is great for the entrepreneur to extend the business into other markets because money could be made. Unfortunately, this is a prescription for mediocrity or outright failure.

Most successful ventures serve a specific market or niche whether it is segmented by industry, geography, market, or technology. They offer unique solutions for very specific customers that have the same specialized interests and needs. The customers in this target market have a strong desire for what the business offers. You need to be sure that your target market is large enough to give you the sales volume you need to make the profits needed to sustain and grow the enterprise, but the target market should be small enough that your competition overlooks it or does not know that it exists.

The most common strategic marketing mistake is to think too big. So, the answer is think small. Think niche. By focusing on a niche, you become expert at providing your product or service. Because you understand the needs of this niche, your marketing message resonates with truth and fit; and your target market buys from you. Your customer is happy because of your expertise and product quality. Your happy customers gladly refer you to other prospective customers who have the same need. This referral process lowers the cost of sales, since you do less prospecting and qualification.

Conversely, the more general your solution and the less specific your customer, the more likely you are to fail. The more you diversify your efforts, the less centered you become. An overly broad charter keeps you from gaining customer knowledge and from gaining operational efficiencies. Your marketing message is weakened by your lack of focus. You get fewer references. Selling is harder and keeping your customers is difficult. Your customers are not as happy.

Niche marketing makes finding the customer easier. You can cull out the customers that don't fit with your plan since not everyone gets the honor of being your customer. Successful niche firms say "no" frequently and don't waste their time on customers that do not fit their niche. The wisdom in knowing what business to avoid is critical to a niche play.

Greater knowledge of your niche allows you to create next-generation products and services. Exploiting a niche allows you greater confidence in your decisions and in your commitments. Your communications with your customers resonate with truth and commitment. Happy customers often will pay higher prices, so you get higher margins and make more money.

I recommend that you find a niche that you feel passionate about. I am not a fan of people launching into a business which does not really interest them. Why do that? Choose a niche that is stimulating or fun or intrigues you. I think the likelihood of success will be much higher if you do what turns you on. It also makes sense to leverage your passion with a niche opportunity where you have special knowledge or special skills. The likelihood of success increases when you leverage these factors; also, it allows you to speak the language used in the niche; in effect, you are one of them.

Some firms stumble into a niche after offering an overly general solution to a broad audience. They find a customer who really needs what they offer and they then start to focus their efforts on that type of customer. They slowly abandon the other customers. This can take a long time and a lot of learning to get this point. This is a typical, but costly, way to find a niche.

To find a new niche, create a concise list of the key differentiating attributes of your current product or service. Compare this list to customers who value these attributes the most. Rank the customers based on their fit with those attributes. Analyze what the highest-ranking customers have in common. Find more customers like these and specialize your offering for them.

Alternatively, you can survey prospective customers to better understand their special needs. This requires active listening on the entrepreneur's part while not leaping to premature conclusions or solutions. This survey exercise should be completed with a representative sample of the market segment; you need to make sure your findings describe the needs of a market big enough for you to make a living in. At this stage, in-person interviews may be the best research method. After doing this preliminary research, you can go back to the same customers with a concept or new product idea; focus groups can be a great way to test new ideas or products. Once again, seek customer feedback so you can validate your product or solution. Move slowly with this research and avoid jumping to conclusions, since understanding your customer is paramount in a niche market.

Consider doing what the big companies pass over or can't be bothered with; do the work that others prefer to outsource. One example would be the shredding of confidential materials, which is a dirty job that large customers don't want to do, but a job that requires a very trustworthy vendor. I have friend in this business and he really cleans up, so to speak.

What to do: Have lunch with a few customers and ask them what they need, but are not getting from their current suppliers. Have them give very specific examples of what they are not getting. Compare the customer needs for similarity.

8. Finding Your Preferred Customer Profile

"Give the public everything you can give them, keep the place as clean as you can keep it, keep it friendly."

Walt Disney (1901–1965) Entrepreneur

For a mature or growing concern, the keys to success may lie under the entrepreneur's nose. After a reasonable period, the enterprise garners a considerable list of customers, some good, some profitable and some a royal pain. I have found that by creating a preferred customer profile, you can audit your existing portfolio of customers to determine your firm's sweet spot.

First, let's come with a list of important factors that describe a good customer:

- Are they located close or far away?
- How far is too far for you to serve them well?
- Are they easy to do business with?
- Do you like them?
- Are they pricing sensitive?
- Do they pay their bills on time?
- What is the likelihood that they will be in business in the future?
- How long have they been a customer?
- How well do they fit with the current product line or service?
- How well will they fit with your future product line or service?
- Have they been a source of referrals?
- How big are they?
- What is their sales volume?
- Do they fit within a certain vertical or industry? If so, which one?
- Etc.

Each factor has a value of 1 to 10. For each customer, assign a value for each factor with 1 being great and 10 being bad. Next, weight these factors by importance on a scale of 1 to 5, with 1 being very important and 5 being very unimportant. For example, with the high cost of shipping, a local customer may be a much better fit for your firm than a customer 500 miles away. A customer that does not pay bills promptly can be a real drag on the P & L (i.e., Profit and Loss Statement), so this might be a factor that is very important.

Once you have designed this measurement tool, let's apply it to all of your customers. This will confirm some basics that you already know and maybe some you don't; at least, this will get them down on paper. Calculate a raw total score for each customer.

The result is a stacked ranking of your customer's fit with your firm. Somewhere in that stack ranking is a line that separates the preferred customers from the expendable customers. My experience tells me that less than 50% of your existing customers will be truly preferred. Obviously, this means that you are wasting your precious resources on a lot of the wrong customers.

OK, here is the smart part and the hard part. What you need to do now is find more customers that fit the preferred customer profile at the top of the stack. Now that you have figured out what your preferred customer looks like, go get more of them.

Brilliant advice you say?

I have been amazed at how many entrepreneurs put up with the aggravation and risk of serving the wrong customers. For some of my clients, the results of this exercise have actually shocked them. I had a client in the shipping materials business that discovered that the non-profit firm, Goodwill Industries International, was by far his preferred customer for a number of reasons: they paid their bills on time, they were local, they were nice people to business with, sales volume was high, and they seldom quibbled about price. Yet, the shipping materials firm had no other customers that even resembled them! Instead, the majority of the other customers were price sensitive, located far away, and generally tough to do business with. Like many small firms, my client was wedded to the cash flow and put up with them. My advice to my client was to find other like non-profits with similar characteristics. I never said that this was rocket science.

My next recommendation may seem obvious, but now that you have determined which customers are preferred, take good care of them. All customers are not the same and you should not treat them the same. Your best customers should be routinely "touched": visited, called, e-mailed, snail mailed, etc. Create a customer calendar with your plan for staying in touch with your best customers. Seek their advice, listen to their concerns, and become friends. These best customers are critical to your success, so let them know how much you appreciate them.

Going forward, I recommend that you focus your marketing efforts on the preferred customers while you abandon your marketing efforts to the customer segments that provide you low-ranking customers. As for the low-ranked customers that you are currently doing business with, you need to fix things. I suggest that you systematically raise prices to prune away the unwanted customers. By raising your prices, you might be able to increase a low ranking customer's score and you might decide you can keep them. If not, you don't want them. Not everybody gets the honor of being your customer.

Getting started: Compile a sales history of your top accounts for the last three years; rank them by volume. What percentage of your total sales do your top customers represent?

9. Market Segmentation: Smaller is Better

"The aim of marketing is to know and understand the customer so well the product or service fits him and sells itself."

Peter Drucker (1909–2005) Educator and writer

Market segmentation is defined as the separating or dividing of a market into sub-groups made up of customers or buyers (i.e., a target market) that require different products or services and thus will require a unique marketing mix. This segmenting of a market into unique sub-segments acknowledges that the sub-segments have common needs, traits, or characteristics. The goal of market segmentation is to maximize your understanding of a customer segment while creating a solution that provides value beyond that of your competition. Your solution is then uniquely positioned in that market segment; this is the customers' perception of how your solution compares to the competition.

Success in today's competitive marketplace is determined increasingly on identifying the subtle differences in a unique market segment so that a firm can have an edge over a competitor. Businesses that sell to a highly segmented subgroup will be more successful; they will be more efficient since they know exactly what the customer wants. Thus, there are no average customers, but rather special customers who desire unique solutions.

For example, firms can segment their market by many factors including:

- Demographics (age, family size, life cycle, occupation)
- Vertical or industry category (consumer, financial, industrial)
- Technology or application or use (Windows, Mac, Unix)
- Geographic (cities, counties, states, regions, countries)
- Behavior (product knowledge, usage, attitudes, responses)
- Psychographic bases (lifestyle, values, personality)

To be successful in your market segmentation, you must target markets that are available to your business and that are big enough for your firm to make a living as a provider. Market segmentation helps the entrepreneur figure out the boundaries of the market. This is not only market size, but also the fit with the customers' needs along with the relationship to the current offerings by the competition.

For the entrepreneur, targeting a unique market segment with few significant competitors creates an opportunity for the firm to provide exceptional value at premium prices. Conversely, the bigger the market you target, the more likely you are to have significant competition; your ability to be intimate with the market will be less and your ability to price on value is diminished.

Someone once said, "There is no such thing as a market. There are only market segments." If that is true, you must think small to be a successful niche marketer.

Food for thought: A segment is only worth serving if it is big enough for you to make a profit.

10. Target Market: Who is Your Customer?

"If you don't know where you're going, you might not get there."

Yogi Berra (1925–) Baseball player

Your target market is the customer group that will buy your product or solution; this specific market is made up of customers who want or need what you're offering. The unique characteristics of your target market will determine the marketing mix (i.e., the 4 Ps or better yet, the 4 Cs).

Historically, marketers have defined target markets using factors or demographics such as age; an example would be such 18- to 33-year-old males. This type of segmentation in the consumer marketplace is now considered inadequate, because of the new sophistication of the consumer and of our increased knowledge of segmentation.

For example, it was commonly thought that someone in their late twenties was an adult, likely married with children, and quickly headed to middle age. Yet, in the new millennium, we find that, while some people in their late twenties fit this profile, many others of the same age group still live at home and have yet to become financially independent; they remain dependent on their parents for financial support. Often, they are unmarried and have no children. Yet, the old segmentation lumps these two disparate groups into one bucket.

We can also describe people by decade or generation, which describes people by age group, but takes into account the experiences that are social, economic, and cultural. This grouping is connected not only by age, but also by what they have witnessed or lived through. Additionally, "cohort marketing", a term originating in consumer marketing circles, defines customer segments using a common experience or multiple experiences shared by a group of people. They have a bond and a common set of needs or interests. For example, Vietnam veterans shared a wartime experience that impacted their lives immeasurably. Another example would be Apple computer users who choose not to follow convention with the Windows operating systems; instead, they take pride in the cult-like creativity and independence that Apple products offer.

So, what does this mean to the entrepreneur? It means that the target market needs to be carefully defined. Your product or solution needs to match precisely with a market segment that wants or needs what you offer.

If you define your market too broadly, you might find yourself with a customer who is indifferent to your offering and may be suspect to move to the competitor that better understands his or her needs.

See the chapter on "Decades".

Think about: What common characteristics or experiences do your customers share? Does your product address those issues?

11. Being First Works Until Something Better Comes Along

"Being First May Not Mean Being Best."

Marc Andreessen (1971–) Netscape cofounder

Being first can be a wonderful thing, until the other guys find out what you are doing. Presuming the market is big enough for more than just your firm, it is likely that the competition has been studying the market opportunity just as long as you have. Only they hesitated to go forward and decided to learn from you.

You were the first one to market. You pioneered your way to market like an adventurer hacking your way through the jungle. Customers have been hard to find since people don't want to take a chance on innovative products or upstart firms. Building your brand awareness was expensive since you were not sure who your customer was and was not; given that uncertainty you threw out a big net to find out what fish you might catch. Product definition was "fuzzy" because of the lack of clarity about the customer needs. What about standards? Heck, you wrote the rules as you went. Looking back, it was easy to underestimate the difficulty of the task.

Now enter the other guys who will save money and time, since they won't have to make the same mistakes that you did. Conveniently for them, you defined the customer opportunity and created the market. Many times the "second-to-market" or "later-to-market" firms make the bigger profits. For example, Apple's iPod was a distant third to Rio and Eiger Labs. Both had fully functioning MP3 players long before the iPod hit the scene. Ever heard of them?

Amazon.com founder Jeff Bezos recently warned his workers "being first isn't necessarily enough." For the entrepreneur in a smaller market, the impact of the second-to-market players may be less of an issue, but the same math still applies. Being first is expensive and difficult. My recommendation for those of you who are first in your market is to quickly move on to being the best or different, since being first is seldom sustainable.

True or false? The first true personal computer was invented by Apple? IBM? Nope. The Altair 8800 was first the first PC; it used an Intel 8080 microprocessor and was sold as a kit in Popular Electronics.

12. Being the Best Takes a Lot of Time, Work, and Money

"The best is the enemy of the good."

Voltaire (1694–1778) Philosopher

The ideal or nirvana for big and small businesses is to be the very best in the eyes of your customer, but it can be exhausting. In the book GOOD TO GREAT, author Jim Collins describes an exhaustive study that his research team did on large companies. His research found that the truly great companies had visionary leaders, had the "right people on the bus", and had unique value propositions. Few large companies made his list of great companies since the costs to get to be number one and stay number one are very high. It takes an outright obsession to be the best and you always live with the fear that everyone else is out to knock you off the top of the hill. The bigger the market and the more competition, the more this is true.

While the same factors exist for the entrepreneur, the benefit to serving a niche market is the lack of competition. This allows the entrepreneur to focus on the customer, rather than constantly looking over your shoulder at the competition. For the entrepreneur to be best, you need to do the following:

- You need to decide what "best" looks like for your customers and remember it is their perception of what is best and important. This definition is your goal.
- You need to recognize that being the best will require a very narrow focus and an intimate knowledge of that market segment. If you don't have the expertise, you can't serve the market, nor can you be the best.
- Your reward for the being best is the undisputed trust of your customer; you get this by making commitments and delivering on them with 100% on-time performance. Being best requires a "zero defects" mentality accepting only excellence in your execution.
- Embracing changes in the marketplace is a fact of life; this recognition sponsors the innovation required to sustain your leadership position. Fighting the inevitable changes in the market is suicide for the entrepreneur.

- Recognize that it is all about people and relationships; although the customer is king, you must acknowledge the importance of your suppliers and your employees. Without their commitment and support, you are only second best.
- You must constantly measure your success against the expectations of your customer. Their satisfaction is the best barometer of your success. This must be routinely monitored.

Question: Can you think of a product or service that is truly the very best? How did you come to that conclusion?

13. Product Differentiation: The Customer's Perception is Everything

"Goober was the type of person who would sit down at a table and say, "Hey, this is great salt.""

Andy Griffith, when describing George Lindsay's character Goober on the Andy Griffith Show (1960–1968)

Being perceived as different in the mind of your customer is critical to a successful niche market strategy. If your customer believes that your product is different and better than the competition, you have achieved product differentiation. This perception is created largely by promotional and marketing strategies, along with the actual differences of your product's features and benefits. However, your product's actual differences are far less important than what the customer thinks is different. This perception is everything.

When you have differentiation, your customer believes that your product is unique when compared to the alternatives. To create this perception, the entrepreneur must create a powerful image that is different from the others. The benefits of product differentiation include a reduction in price sensitivity, increased brand loyalty, and longer product life cycles.

To create this differentiation, here are a few basics requirements:

- Your customer must really need the product; all the differentiation in the world won't help you sell a product that is not truly desired or needed.
- Your product's features and benefits must be viewed as valuable, unique, or special. This means that you must differentiate your product based on factors that are important to the customer such as quality, performance, prestige, or reliability.
- The customer needs to be able to measure the differences between your product and the competition; if all the competitors say that their product is highest in quality, keying your product differentiation on quality would be a "me too" play and likely be ineffective.

For a niche marketer, you need to create differentiation that is sustainable over the long term and defensible against the competition. Superior service would be a good example of differentiation that can be sustained. Nordstrom, the high-end retailer, has distinguished itself with superior customer service while pricing at a premium. Nordstrom has successfully defended this positioning for decades. An example of unsustainable product differentiation would be a "lowest price" strategy; this type of strategy would not be defensible for a niche player since there is inevitably a competitor dumb enough or desperate enough to offer an even lower price.

Here are some ways to differentiate your product from the competition:

- Appeal to the buyer's emotions. Consumer products often create images that pull at the "heart strings" of buyers. For example, many "comfort" food products use advertising campaigns that play on nostalgia. For B2B (business to business) products, fear can be a powerful motivator.
- Product or service guarantees can be powerful differentiators when the competition does not offer them; unfortunately, this type of differentiator tends to be a "follow-the-leader" tactic and is not often sustainable.
- By focusing on a specific market segment with unique needs, you can create a new product category. This is the essence of niche marketing and can be sustainable due to the segment's small size and your superior knowledge. An example of this would be a retailer of record albums in the era of compact discs and MP3s. A small segment of music buyers prefer the higher fidelity found on albums pressed the old-fashioned way on vinyl. I was in such a store in Chicago that specialized in vinyl records; I was amazed to see contemporary music still released on vinyl but at three times the price of the comparable compact disc.
- Pricing differently can be a differentiator; for example, you can price a service using a flat rate while others price using variable pricing formulas. Netflix.com, the online video rental service, charges a monthly flat rate for video rentals while the competition charges a fee for individual video rentals and also charges for late returns. As powerful as this strategy is, the competitor can easily clone it.
- Bundling-in other products or services can be a powerful differentiator. For example, Hollywood Video, the video retailer, packages its in-store rentals with candy, popcorn, and soft drinks. The message to the consumer is to make renting videos a party.

- While some providers may rely upon the ignorance of the buyer, a successful niche marketer needs to communicate the unique differences of the product when compared to the competition. This requires the use of carefully written advertising copy, along with persuasive brochures and packaging.
- Packaging can get the customer's attention; this is helped by using bright colors and good visuals including professional photography. The benefits of the product need to be quickly discerned, while the packaging itself must be memorable.
- The name of the product can be critical to a product's success and differentiation. In the book business, book titles must be catchy or even outrageous to get the book buyer's attention. If a book does not sell well, publishers sometimes will remarket the book under a different title. The publishing industry has thousands of examples of successful books remarketed a second time with a new name.
- Quality is strong differentiator and often very defensible. For the customer, quality can be measurable and is worth a premium price. This differentiator presumes superior quality for your product when compared to the competitor. In addition, this presumes that the buyer wants and needs superior quality.
- Location or availability can be a differentiator. An example of this would be the pervasiveness of McDonald's. The convenience and consistency offered by this fast food chain makes for a sustainable differentiator since McDonald's is located everywhere on the planet, or so it seems.
- Advertising images can create strong differentiation in the customer's eyes. Admittedly, this can be costly, but once created can create real barriers to entry for the competition. This type of differentiation is often done with high-end products such as exotic cars, perfumes, or clothing. BMW has spent millions of dollars on advertising to create an image of performance and prestige for the automobile buyer.

Homework assignment: Create a list of all the things different about your product when compared to your competitors. Next time that you are with a loyal customer, ask them the same question. Compare the lists.

14. Don't Hide From the Competition

"Know your enemy, and in one hundred battles you will never be defeated."

Sun Tzu (544–496 A.D.) Chinese military strategist

Most of the successful small firms that I have studied have successfully positioned themselves in a market segment where they have little significant competition. This allows room for a decent profit margin and focuses the firm's efforts on pleasing the customer, while not on worrying about what the competition will do next. Invariably these firms are continuous innovators.

The problem that I have with hiding from competitors is that you may also be hiding from customers. Let me tell you that it is hard to create a market for a new product or service. Innovation is cool, but it requires a special customer who wants to be innovative, too. You can burn a lot of rubber trying to find that innovative customer. If you cannot find any competitors who are making money in your market segment, you may want to ask yourself if there is really a business there anyway.

Another approach that is successful and can provide a possible exit down the road is to compete against big and dumb companies or institutions. Competing against smart competitors can be hard; when they have seemingly endless resources, it can be lethal. Big and dumb firms allow you the chance to steal their customers without their even knowing it since your firm is so small by comparison. To do so requires specialization that your customer values.

The best example of big and dumb that I can think of is the U.S. Postal Service. Two centuries of tradition and bureaucracy have made the U.S. Postal Service one of the most lethargic and disconnected institutions on earth. By providing a similar service without the lethargy and bureaucracy, FedEx grew into a marketing giant. FedEx delivers the next day with greater than 99% accuracy, which is something that the U.S. Postal Service still cannot figure out.

You can see that when competing with big and dumb competitors you might get access to a real customer base and make a nice living. By the time the big and dumb firms find out about you, your company has prospered and grown to such an extent that the big and dumb competitor might just have to buy you out at a premium. Name your own price because as you know, they are big and dumb.

Question: What large companies overlook small segments that fit your solution? Why?

15. The Zen of Marketing

"Words have the power to both destroy and heal. When words are both true and kind, they can change our world."

Buddha (565–455 B.C.) Religious leader

OK, I am out on tree limb here, but hang with me for minute. Let's look at marketing from a Zen Master's perspective. People all aspire to be happy since it is our common purpose. This also applies to companies, which are just formal groupings of people who also want to be happy. Zen tells us that whether the customer is an individual, a small business, or a multi-national corporation, they all make purchasing decisions to make life better one decision at a time.

Many of today's marketing campaigns are fear based and negative; the message to the customer is buy the product or you will suffer horribly or be in great pain. Think I am kidding? It was not that long ago that American Express proclaimed, "Don't leave home without it". I am not sure what bad thing was going to happen, but it must have been really bad for them to spend all that money warning us about it. How about the mouthwash campaigns? The message is clear that if you don't use mouthwash, you will have no friends.

Rather than repeatedly threatening your prospective customer with fear-filled messages, try telling them to stop worrying and be happy. Let them know that your firm can be trusted and that you can ease their pain. Explain how your solution can save time and money. Focus on the benefits you will offer them.

Think of the most successful brands today. They seldom speak of products or features, rather they tell you how the product or service will make you feel. Coca-Cola makes life fun and enjoyable. Volvo makes you feel safe. Nike challenges you to strive to new heights (and they never mention tennis shoes). All these world-class brands send a positive message about making you happier.

A positive message makes the sender more appealing or attractive than a negative message. Send a positive message by practicing the following:

- Never speak ill of the competition; I find it best to avoid using a competitor's name at all. If the customer asks you about the competition, I suggest responding with, "I cannot speak for the competition, but at our firm, we focus on…."

- Focus your product messaging on the benefits of your solutions and how they will make your customer feel better.
- Eliminate negative marketing campaign messages since they are perceived as demeaning; dragging someone else down to make you look good is the behavior of a bully or someone with an inferiority complex. The same applies to companies.
- Don't gossip. It is the lowest form of networking and reflects poorly on your brand and you.
- Event marketing can be a terrific way for your firm to showcase your successes; major positive events don't come along often, so make the most of them.
- Associate your firm with charitable causes; receive positive publicity by giving back to the community or to a charity. (See the chapter called "Cause Marketing: Do Good and Get Rewarded For It".)
- Audit your website; read it as a customer would. Does it send a positive message? If not, correct it.
- Avoid sarcasm in e-mails. This one is hard for me, since I love a good joke. However, you never know who the reader is going to be and how they will interpret your snide or sarcastic remark. It is better to be safe than sorry.
- Public relations are tricky since you cannot control what the media will actually say. When talking to the media focus your comments on the subject and don't get derailed by wondering off subject and getting quoted on something sensational. A wise friend of mine told me that when talking to the press, you should be a drinking fountain, not a fire hose.
- Include evidence of your customers' happiness with testimonials on your website and in your brochures. Tie the testimonials to your product benefits.

Don't worry. Be happy.

Action item: Ask your customers what factors or features make them satisfied with a supplier or service provider. Are these factors or features part of your solution?

16. Sustainable Competitive Advantage: Be Different

"You either have to be first, best, or different."

Loretta Lynn (1935–) Country western singer

Another common phrase used in marketing circles is "sustainable competitive advantage" (often abbreviated as SCA). Michael Porter, lauded Professor of Harvard University, coined the term. SCA is a description of what is unique about your product or solution that makes you valued in the marketplace. A competitive advantage is sustainable if others can't copy or deliver the same thing, or if the cost or the time to develop a competing solution is very significant. Porter suggests that a competitive advantage is achieved when you do different things that are valued by your customer and are not available from the competition. Alternatively, you can create a competitive advantage by doing things differently, which are valued by the customer and are not available from the competition.

For example, Apple created the iPod, which allowed the consumer to inexpensively download music on a mobile device. We can debate whether they were first (they were not), and whether this advantage is sustainable (probably not), but Apple did create the MP3 movement for the mass consumption market. This is an example of doing something different. On the other hand, Starbucks sells coffee, which is not exactly a new product, but Starbucks markets coffee in a different way than others have. They market "premium coffee", whatever that is. Moreover, they charge a premium for this difference. Thus, Starbucks is an example of how you can achieve a competitive advantage by doing something differently.

In some industries, being first allows for a competitive advantage, but seldom is it sustainable in the long run. Invariably the word gets out and the competition joins the market erasing whatever advantage there was for the first entry. Apple was enormously innovative with their early personal computers which offered a graphical user interface and a mouse. IBM later entered the market and grabbed market share; all Apple could do was watch.

I have found that specialization in a niche for a business helps ensure the sustainability of the competitive advantage. This specialization is achieved by having expert knowledge of the target market; by fully understanding the wants and needs of the customer, your offering is better than the other competitors. This can be true if your product is different or you do things differently. A wise man once said, "Only dead fish swim with the current"; for a niche business, there may be nothing more important than being different or doing things differently. Being the same as your competition is a dead-end street littered with price reductions, canceled orders, and missed sales forecasts.

Not surprisingly, I have witnessed that a tight geographic focus helps create a strong competitive advantage for niche businesses; the sheer constraint on geography allows for excellence and bars competitors from getting a toehold. This goes counter to the thinking of many entrepreneurs who are tempted to stretch their geographical boundaries for additional cash flow.

Participating in a niche market with few competitors helps create sustainable competitive advantage. With fewer competitors, the provider can capture higher margins and profits, which allow the entrepreneur to invest more in the firm.

Of course, brilliant designs that are patented can provide competitive advantages, but in our global economy, patents are increasingly difficult to defend. Talk to someone who competes with Asian firms in a global market and you will find that good ideas or products are quickly cloned. Catch them if you can.

Question for you to answer: What is your sustainable competitive advantage?

17. Why Do Market Research When I Talk With My Customers All the Time?

"There are three kinds of lies: lies, damned lies, and statistics."

Benjamin Disraeli (1804–1881) British politician

Most entrepreneurs make decisions based on past experiences, along with logic and feel. When you get down to it, who knows better about what to do for the business than the entrepreneur? When it comes to understanding the customers' attitudes, preferences, and opinions, the same thinking is frequently applied.

This "by the gut" approach can work a big part of the time, but we all have blind spots in our thinking. These blind spots are based on past experiences and our learning from them. We tend to learn from our mistakes early in life and adjust our behavior accordingly. For example, as a child you are told that the stove is hot, but often you don't really learn that the stove is hot until you touch it and get burned. A few repetitions of this and you will get it: the stove is hot. OK, don't touch the stove. From that point on, all stoves are determined to be hot. We are careful. This is now fact. This thinking helps us to not get burned again.

Blind spots can also make us blind to opportunity or truth. In a way similar to the hot stove, we can learn to be prejudiced or overly judgmental. For instance, a bad dining experience at a restaurant might keep you from going back; the restaurant could hire one the best cooks in the country, but you still will remember the bad food and probably won't go back.

This tendency towards bias applies to market research. As entrepreneurs, we think we know what our customers want or feel; after all, we talk with them all the time. Alternatively, some entrepreneurs are inventors of new products or technologies; they often need to find customers who will want the new inventions. Market research is a way to confirm the customers' view of things and to learn new things that we did not know about our products or services. It is because of our blind spots that we need to do market research. Market research confirms what we know and can also tell us what we don't.

Action: Next time a market research firm calls you at home, don't hang up. Instead, listen carefully to the questions they ask. Visualize the interviewer reading the questions; is the interviewer really listening to the answers?

18. Market Research Methods: How to Get Started

"We know what we are, but know not what we may be."

William Shakespeare (1564–1616) Playwright

The best way to begin your market research is to first check for pertinent secondary research; this is research already completed and written. Examples of secondary research include newspapers, magazines, journals and syndicated research such as reports or newsletters. Often this research is inexpensive or free and it is up to you find it. Sources for this research could include the internet, libraries, trade associations, and market research firms. Invariably this type of research may be helpful in sizing your market for your new product, but it probably will not be as specific as you will need. Seldom will secondary research confirm customer views about your product, but it remains a good way to start the research process.

Here's a tip: if you can buy secondary market research on your niche, the niche is probably too big. If a market is big enough for a research firm or magazine to analyze it, then it means there probably are many competitors out there that are interested in getting that research. Niche markets usually don't warrant the attention of research firms or magazines. The lack of good secondary research will challenge the entrepreneur to pursue custom research, also known as primary research.

Primary research should first begin with qualitative research. Using open-ended questions, qualitative research is like a fishing expedition. You know that you will likely catch fish, but you don't know when the fish will bite, what type of bait that the fish will bite, or how many fish you will catch, never mind what type of fish you will catch. Examples of qualitative research include focus groups (more on that later) and interviews. These techniques look to identify what is important and why these things are important.

Qualitative interviews ask the respondent open-ended questions; this can be done in-person or on the phone. The trick is not to bias the answers by unnecessarily agreeing or disagreeing with the respondent. The best approach is to ask every respondent the exact same question in exactly the same manner, while divorcing your personal opinions or feelings from the process.

In-person interviews tend to be more costly, but can be very in-depth.

The interviewer can typically spend more time with the respondent, sometimes up to an hour. The respondent can review materials or products, while the interviewer can monitor body language. The interviewer can ask closed-ended or open-ended questions which can allow exploration of opinions.

One type of in-person interview, which can be very effective, is called an "intercept" interview. This type of in-person survey is great for consumer research. The technique is simple. You stand in front a high traffic area such as a consumer electronics store and you snag people as they come and go from the store. Alternatively, you can approach people at a shopping mall and request to meet with them in a private office. Typically, you can only keep your respondent for up to ten minutes; offering an incentive might get the respondent to talk longer. The expected response rate can be as high as 50%, which is great. This technique can be good for testing new products, new packaging, or for naming new products. Again, this method is best suited for B2C (business to consumer) research.

Telephone interviews are cheaper to conduct than in-person interviews. Additionally, telephone interviews allow you to easily accommodate a diverse geographical cross section of respondents who can be randomly selected. Telephone interviews seldom last more than ten minutes unless financial incentives are offered.

After you have completed your qualitative research, the next step is to test your findings using quantitative research. Often the findings from your in-person interviews are interesting and may yield great directional feedback for making product or service decisions; but they are not statistically representative of what your target market truly thinks. To be sure, you need to survey a representative sample of your customers to verify the qualitative research findings. Using closed-end questions via mail or phone or e-mail, you can verify what your target market really thinks and feels about your solution or idea. This type of research can be very powerful and definitive.

Mail survey research is a time-proven method of gathering research. A carefully crafted questionnaire can be mailed to a geographically diverse audience at a relatively low cost. Mail surveys work well for sensitive questions that might be hard to handle in-person or over the phone. Response rates are notoriously low with a 5% response rate considered high. Mail surveys can drag on for weeks, since there is little incentive for the respondent to hurry. Cost is modest, but more expensive than web-based market research. Some researchers will argue that mail surveys are passé and have been replaced by online surveys due to the lower costs offered by the internet. Still, mail surveys may be a good way to reach some types of respondents, such as older people or people who shun personal computers. For example, Hispanics are a major purchasing force in the U.S., but they have lower PC adoption rates than Caucasians. Mail surveys, along with phone survey techniques, might prove a better research method to reach them.

Web-based market research offers a low-cost approach and has proven to be effective despite the one-dimensional communication of the keyboard and the mouse. Website visitors are often invited to do e-mail surveys via pop-ups. Internet-based research is very inexpensive since you have no mailing costs and no interviewers. A weakness to this approach is the very low response rate.

For a startup, "concept testing" a new product or idea can save time and money. Surprisingly, most new ventures crash forward without testing new ideas or products. Concept testing is a gut-level check with key customers to verify that your solution has merit; the first-round check might be with a few friends or loyal customers. A second check should be with another round of customers, who might not be as a loyal. This pre-launch probing could avert a marketing disaster and wasted money.

A low-cost idea for market research would be to hire an intern from the local university to conduct the research in your behalf. Give them a script and a phone and let them dial away, gathering the information that you don't have time to get. They will love the real-world experience and you will be amazed at what your customers will share (without you there).

Your action: Call the local university or college business school and ask them about how to get a college intern to help you with your marketing.

19. Focus Groups Help You Fish For Answers

"Give me six hours to chop down a tree and I will spend the first four sharpening the axe."

Abraham Lincoln (1809–1865) President

The purpose of a focus group is to help find answers to difficult questions. A consumer-research technique that uses open-ended questions, focus groups can quickly discern key issues and determine why the issues are important. Focus groups are moderator-led discussions of six to ten people randomly selected from a sample list comprised of participants in your target market.

An independent, third party moderator who is trained at managing the complex interpersonal dynamics of a group discussion best conducts "true" focus groups. The goal of a focus group is to smoke out hidden issues, test ideas, and seek feedback from the participants on topics such advertising, new products, or customer needs. The group discussion environment can be a very powerful tool for determining how people feel about the topic.

The client who sponsors the focus group predetermines the objectives of the session, but the format is flexible enough to accommodate the serendipity of qualitative research. You never know exactly what you will learn in a focus group. Most moderators prefer to follow a discussion outline, but they let the discussion lead the way. A typical discussion outline for a new product or concept often will have a format as follows:

Introduction of the Issue or Problem

- Define the issue or problem.
- Confirm the group's understanding about the issue or the problem.
- Reconfirm that individuals in the group do not have conflicts of interest.

Discuss the Current Situation or Environment

- What products are currently available?
- How are the current products being used today?
- What is the current satisfaction with the available products?
- What are the biggest problems with these products?
- What is working well today?
- What key needs are unaddressed?

Competitive Analysis

- Confirm the awareness of key vendors.
- Solicit reactions to key vendors.
- Rank strengths and weaknesses of each vendor.

New Product or Concept Introduced

- Solicit group reactions to the new product or concept.
- Review the product definition.
- Review the need for the product,
- Review the strengths/weaknesses of the new product.
- Review the decision process for the new product.

Once the focus group discussion outline is written, the moderator and the client typically write a discussion guide, which is a list of questions that follows the objectives in the discussion outline. This is a tool to keep the moderator and the group on track. The focus group participants are recruited randomly from a sample provided by the client; typically, job titles are a key factor in this recruitment. For example, CIOs (Chief Information Officers) are highly prized participants in a focus group on software. Often the CIOs will need an incentive to participate; incentives can range from $200 to $300 (or more) depending on the seniority of the participants. Focus groups usually last between one to two hours and are often done at lunch or in the early evenings. When the focus group is held at a professional focus group facility, the sponsoring party can watch the focus group live via a two-way mirror and listen via microphones and speakers. To avoid a regional bias with focus groups, multiple groups are often held in different locations such as San Francisco, Dallas, and New York. The focus groups are video taped for later review.

Recently, online focus groups have been used to gain access to respondents who might not normally attend in-person focus groups; online groups are flexible and low cost. Online focus group findings can be very reliable if carefully recruited; a weakness of early online focus group efforts was reliability due to ad hoc sampling (not being careful about who was chosen to participate). With careful sampling, online focus groups can be very reliable. An advantage of online focus groups would be the ability to incorporate geographic diversity with respondents from all over the world. Additionally, most online focus groups are done at the convenience of the respondent, which allows for a more complete discussion.

A focus group that is poorly or unprofessionally moderated is a waste of time. Generally speaking, focus groups are best left to the professionals. Often small firms will attempt to moderate focus groups by themselves; this is often a poor choice since the entrepreneurs are inherently biased (or, call it passionate) about their businesses and will only hear what they want to hear. True focus groups can be cost prohibitive; focus groups done with a professional moderator can cost $6,000–10,000 per group.

Alternatively, you can hire a non-professional moderator to reduce the cost. Keep in mind that the non-professional moderator needs to be unbiased and cannot be an employee of the sponsoring firm. The focus group should be held at a neutral location away from the sponsoring company facilities.

Consider this: Hire a local psychologist to moderate the group, recruit the participants yourself, coach the psychologist on the questions to ask, conduct it at your facility, and videotape it yourself. This will keep the costs down and keep your bias out.

20. Competitive Analysis: It's a Dog-Eat-Dog World

"It's not the size of the dog in the fight; it's the size of the fight in the dog."

Mark Twain (1835–1910) Author and wit

If you are targeting a market with many competitors, it is highly likely that you are not targeting a niche market since a successful provider in a niche market has few competitors, if any. This raises the question, why do competitive analysis?

Competitive analysis is important even if you have only one or two competitors; your sustainable competitive advantage and your value-based pricing are directly tied to your uniqueness. If your competitor is attempting to copy your offering, you could be in big trouble. The other instance when competitive analysis applies to a niche market would be when existing suppliers overlook or choose not to serve a segment of the market, thus creating your opportunity. In this case, you will need to monitor them closely; they might change their minds after they see your continued success.

Doing competitive analysis is easy, but time consuming. The objective is to gather information about the competitor on an ongoing basis that will tell the story about their strategy, goals, and anticipated behavior. Here are a few things that you will want to know about your competitors:

- What products or services does your competitor offer?
- What are their product specifications, data sheets, brochures, and samples?
- Who are their major customers?
- What types of customers do business with them?
- How do their customers feel about them as a provider?
- Have they lost any major customers? If so, why?
- What are their channels of distribution?
- Do they use direct sales, agents, distributors, etc?
- What is their competitive advantage?
- What is the reputation of your competitor?
- How are they different from other firms?
- How are they different from your firm?
- What prices to they charge?

- What is their pricing strategy?
- Do they offer discounts?
- What terms do they offer?
- What is their advertising message?
- Where do they choose to advertise?
- Who is their PR firm?
- Where are their locations?
- Number of employees?
- Fiscal year end?
- Union or non-union?
- On-time performance?
- Have any complaints been filed with industry reporting agencies such as the State Contractors Board or the Better Business Bureau?
- What trade shows do they attend?
- What organizations do they support?
- Who works for them? Who does what? What does their organization chart look like?
- Do they have any affiliates or partner organizations?
- How is their financial health?
- What are their estimated annual sales?
- Who are their key investors?
- Do they pay their bills on time?
- Have they had a lay off recently?
- Do they have any job openings?
- Key executives names and experience?
- What is the competitor's website like?

I think you get the picture. Just about any information you can gather can help you better understand the competitor, how they think, and where they are going. Key in this research is the gathering of information on an ongoing basis and checking its accuracy. Old competitive information is largely worthless, since it may have no bearing on where they might be headed in the future. False or unreliable information is obviously no good. It makes good sense to double-check all information by seeking verification from an insider such as a current customer or seek a second source of information that complements the first piece gathered. An example of that would be if you hear from one customer that your competitor offered a new product; seek a confirmation from another customer which may have heard about or seen the new product.

Here are a few ways to gather information:

- Network at industry events; people love to gossip and you can listen to them after you ask an open-ended question like, "Have you heard that ZXY opened a new plant in Salem?"
- Talk with the suppliers to your competitors; often suppliers will be intimate with your competitors' financial health, new products, and strategies. Seldom are they loyal enough to keep this good stuff a secret. All is fair. Note the lesson: beware of what you tell your suppliers.
- Look for secondary research about your competitors in the local papers, industry publications, and in trade journals. Consider looking through back issues.
- Do a search on Google. The internet is full of information, but beware that just because it is on the internet does not make it correct.
- Visit the competitors' websites; you will be amazed how some firms will "spill their guts" on their website. They may list customers, pricing, testimonials and press releases; this can be very convenient for doing research. Another lesson: never put anything on your website that you don't want to share with a competitor.
- Talk to former employees of competitors; sometimes they sing like canaries. This particularly applies to unhappy former employees. Beware of confidentiality agreements. Stay ethical. Stay within the law. This is research not espionage.
- Check out court records; if there was a lawsuit, this is public information. If you have never read the proceedings from a trial, I recommend that you check this out. Any question is fair in court, or so it seems. Court records can be very revealing and very entertaining.
- Consider doing a background check on the competitor's executives; you might find out some interesting stuff that might explain some erratic behavior. This is perfectly legal.
- Talk to their sales reps; some reps can't help themselves from spilling the beans. They can tell you what happened last year, along with what the plans are for the future.
- Check out online databases, if they exist for your industry. Industry associations may be a good place to start.
- Do a "D & B (Dun and Bradstreet) check" on your competitor. D & B profiles large and small companies; they publish facts gathered directly from the firms profiled including number of employees, revenues, facility locations, etc. Check out what was reported to this data-gathering firm. I have always found it

funny that the competitor will give information to D & B with no questions asked, but will withhold this type of information from others.

- Put someone in charge of competitive intelligence; it is an important job.

Your action: Create a file folder on your PC and add a file folder in your desk for competitive information. Save every bit of competitive information you find. Ask everyone in your company to send what they find to you; if you are too busy, assign it to one your staff members. This is an ongoing task.

21. How to Do Customer Satisfaction Surveys

"You can't just ask customers what they want and then try to give that to them. By the time you get it built, they'll want something new."

Steve Jobs (1955–) Founder of Apple Computer

Most entrepreneurs talk with their customers and have done so for a long time, so they know exactly what their customers think and feel. At least they think they do.

The same applies for salespeople. You rely on your salespeople to communicate with your customers and to listen for feedback. Most salespeople are good at this, but they sometimes hear only what they want to hear, while the customers only tell the sales people what they want to tell them. Missing from this dialog is how customers really feel about your product or service, how they feel about doing business with your firm, and if they intend to continue doing business with your firm. Remember that it is the salesperson's job to sell existing products and services. This focus on the here and now is warranted; it is for this reason, that the salesperson doesn't get the full story from the customer.

This is why a firm with a niche market focus needs to do continuous customer satisfaction research. Customer needs are not static. In fact, their needs evolve and change continuously, which requires the entrepreneur to innovate and respond quickly. If you don't change and adapt, there is a good chance that your competitor will. Waiting to change later may be too late.

The methods for obtaining this information include direct mail, e-mail, telephone, in-person, and website surveys, to name a few. Whatever method, I recommend that you ask your customers the following basic questions:

- Why do they choose to do business with your firm?
- What do they like and dislike about doing business with your firm?
- How is your product or service similar or different from the competition?
- What do they like most about your product or service?
- What do they like least about your product or service?

- Would they recommend your firm to a friend or colleague?
- Have they recommended your firm to a friend or colleague?

I prefer to do anonymous surveys, which allow the customer to comment more freely. This will favor a third party administering surveys if it is over the phone, or it will favor written surveys. Ask simple questions that focus on one subject; you often get what you ask for, so be precise in your questionnaire design. Be sure to add variety to your questions, since survey questions can all sound alike to the respondent.

I also prefer to survey continuously rather than once a year since a lot can happen in one year. One way to survey continuously is to attach a customer survey postcard to your invoices; if you bill them frequently, you may choose to do this every quarter. Or have a button on your website called "How Are We Serving You?" Compile the results and look for trends. Fix what is wrong. Don't delay.

Your to do list: Google the words "customer satisfaction" and see the different techniques for gathering this type of information.

22. Pricing Your Products
to Make Money

"Money is better than poverty, if only for financial reasons."

Woody Allen (1935–) Comedian, actor, and director

Pricing may be the most important decision that the entrepreneur makes. Often this decision is rushed and done by the seat of the pants. Most entrepreneurs think pricing is easy.

Many small businesses use mark-up pricing. Mark-up pricing uses some multiple of cost such as three or four times the "estimated cost". The entrepreneur says, "If it costs a dollar to make the widget, I need to sell it for three or four dollars. Hey baby, we are living large!" Whoops! Look back a few words and you will see the word "estimated"; most entrepreneurs don't know what their actual costs truly are. Often they under price their products since cost accounting at small firms is only the sum of direct materials and direct labor, if that.

Competitive pricing is even more scientific. Simply, you price your product or service to be just below competition or to match a competitor's price. Why? Is the competitor down the street a pricing genius to be reckoned with? I think not. I guess this approach presumes that the competitor is the price leader and has educated all customers to this price. My guess is that the competitor may have used a crystal ball or had his cousin Vinny price his product. Fallible? You bet. This pricing method is used at large and small firms.

At a start up, first-time customers may deserve special pricing to compensate them for the risk of doing business with the new enterprise. So quote them two prices: charter or founder prices for today and a standard price or list price for a year from now, which they will ultimately have to pay. A weakness of this method is that once you give a price to a customer, it is very hard to raise prices after that. This approach is best used at the earliest introduction of a product or service for a start-up while you don't have many customers. Be careful.

"Perceived value-based" pricing is pricing for a product or service at a level that reflects the potential savings, the highest satisfaction level, or the maximum use that a client will receive from the purchase and the use of the product or service. Overall, price is set at the highest level that your target market is willing to pay, given these benefits. This type of pricing reflects a sustainable competitive advantage where there is little or no competition. This is niche market heaven. However, be sure that your competitive advantage is real and defensible, or you have got trouble on the way. How much is too much to charge, when utilizing perceived value based pricing? Look for tearstains on the checks you receive from customers. If it hurts them to write you a check, then you are charging too much. If that is the case, you won't keep them as customers for long.

"Skimming" refers to pricing a new product at a high level while you can. This is a market where a competitive advantage may not be sustainable. Most often, this is used in a market that is big enough to attract new competition. This happens a great deal in technology when an innovative product first captures the customer's attention. One reason to set an initial high price is to establish the new product as a prestige or a high quality product; by beginning with a high price, you also have room to move down in price with the anticipated entrance of competition. This is not the pricing strategy for a niche player since a niche-pricing strategy is based on a sustainable competitive advantage and a partnership with the customer. An example of skimming would be the DVR (digital video recorder) product called TiVo, which has revolutionized watching television. Early on, this was a product for the early adopters and TiVo products commanded a premium price. Competition entered the market and prices softened. Soon all satellite receivers will have DVR features. Game over.

"Penetration" pricing is a tactic where a provider sells below market price to break into a market or to take market share. This is what the Japanese semiconductor makers did in the 1980's; buoyed by a lower cost of capital and a government-sponsored long-term objective, taking market share from the U.S. semiconductor firms was the worth the short-term losses. You may recall that the U.S. manufacturers called foul on this practice and referred to it as "dumping". Japan emerged as a major player in the semiconductor memory chip business and pushed many U.S. suppliers out of the business. This is a very interesting tactic, but hardly a tool for entrepreneurs like you and me.

"Economic or mass market" pricing is used when margins are slim, volumes are high, and there are many competitors. The best example of this may be in the grocery business. Economic pricing is highly elastic with slight pricing variances creating major swings in demand. This type of pricing does apply to a niche market and is not for us to be bothered with in this book. Sorry Safeway.

The point to remember is that cost is to value as fish are to bicycles (i.e., there is no real relationship). As a niche player with a sustainable competitive advantage, you always want to price your product or solution using a perceived value pricing methodology. If you cannot price in this fashion you are not a niche marketer.

You must do this: Keep a log of all the prices quoted to customers. Include the customer names, date, amount and the reason for the discount, if offered. Keep a log of competitive pricing including customer name, date, and amount.

23. *Give it Away to Get Your Business Started*

"Of all sad words of tongue and pen, the saddest are these…
what might have been."

William Shakespeare (1564–1616) Playwright

Do business pro bono.

"Pro bono" is a Latin phrase, which means "for the good". For some new business efforts, you have to give it away if you want to get your business started. The alternative might be no business at all. You might get started by giving it away to your friends and family and colleagues. Free or not, these first customers can function as your reference accounts and might help you debug or improve your product.

Free consultations with prospective customers are a great way to get relationships started. Offer the consultation for a limited period of time (Thirty minutes might be too short, so generally I suggest a hour.) and one time only. The consultation should focus on the customer needs or problem and they should do most of the talking. Oddly enough, I recommend that you resist the urge to sell. Rather, focus the conversation on the customer and their issues. Offer your advice and counsel on the options available. I suggest that you speak to them as you would to a friend, since creating the relationship is your first objective. Conclude the meeting by thanking them for the chance to talk and let them know how to contact you. Ask their permission to be added to your mail list. Finally, follow up with a personal note card. This technique is very powerful since it so low key and customer focused. It is my experience that they generally call you back to talk about your services.

The same approach works with small groups. Offer a free seminar in person, on the phone, or via a webinar (a telephone conference with a PowerPoint presentation). Admittedly, the group format loses some of its intimacy, but it can be an effective way to get your message out. I have a friend who is an investment advisor; he specializes in helping teachers for grades kindergarten through twelve with rollovers of 403B tax deferred savings plans (Note his highly-focused niche!). Knowing that teachers are busy all day during the week and are grading papers and tests in the evenings, he hosts Saturday morning breakfast seminars on investment topics of general interest. Typically, he gets a group of ten to fifteen teachers for the seminar and breakfast; he positions himself as a knowledge broker and talks eloquently on an investment topic. The whole affair is over in 90 minutes with many of the teachers asking for an appointment to discuss their rollover needs. This is a very powerful technique.

If you are in the service business, free trials are a great way to create new customers. One technique that I have seen used effectively is to offer the first month of your service free. Make sure that the service delivered is top notch during the trial. At the end of the month, a one-year agreement is offered with payment due net 30. In effect, you entered into a thirteen-month agreement with net 60 terms and 30-day cancellation clause. If your service matches the customers' needs, the trial can begin a long-term relationship.

Giving it away can create relationships, get you references, and sell your products. Everybody wins.

Try it this month: Offer free samples or a free trial as a new promotion.

24. Branding is a Promise of Value

"Create your own style. Let it be unique for yourself
and yet identifiable for others."

Orson Welles (1915–1985) Author, actor, director

Your brand is what people think you are. It answers the questions, "How you are expert?", "How are you different?", and "Why are you valued?" Successful brands are authentic, differentiated, and consistent.

Brands are authentic when they are real and natural. Fabricated brands seldom live for long. No pretense or fibs allowed here. You cannot make up a brand since a brand must have integrity to be believed. When a brand is based on falsehoods or exaggerations, no one will believe you, nor will they continue to buy from you. Not for long anyway.

Brands are differentiated when they say what is unique or special about the business or product. A differentiated brand answers why and how the firm delivers value. A good brand describes what makes your firm different from the competition. It describes the uniqueness of your product; this is what the customer remembers.

Consistency is the commitment from the brand that the purchase experience will be the same each time. Otherwise, why would anyone buy the same product or service again? Consistency allows the brand to live on beyond the first impression; the hope for the brand is that it will take on a life of its own. Brands can actually outlive the firm or the product. Your target customer knows that each purchase will be the same as the last. Successful brands are reliable.

Your brand is a promise of value that separates you from your peers. Branding is not about building a new image, but it is a statement about your uniqueness. Successful brands know their target market; they know what the customer needs. They deliver.

So, what are the benefits of the brand you ask?

A vibrant brand helps the customer understand better what your firm is all about. A stellar brand will increase visibility and presence while differentiating your business from the competition. Selling is made easier with repeat customers who buy with confidence since they understand the brand. Customers trust that your product or service will be the same every time. Every customer contact with your firm builds your brand awareness and reinforces the message. Brand loyalty increases with each successful interaction with the brand.

Finally, for brands to have longevity they must evolve (while remaining consistent and true). As your market changes, so must your brand change. Brands must be relevant and must live in the present tense. Aging brands that don't evolve and cling to the past will eventually lose their relevance. Brands stay relevant by changing as the market changes. McDonald's now serves salads in response to changing food habits. Technically, this is called line extension; this is when you add new products or features. For McDonald's, this continued relevance of the brand helps ensure its longevity. McDonald's is more than just burgers and fries today; they also post nutritional information at the counter. The brand has evolved to stay relevant.

To stay relevant, you can augment your brand with new attributes. A good example is Volvo, long known for safety and crashworthiness, which now has cachet (at least, some people think so). For Volvo, their brand has become more complex and inclusive in response to the changing automobile market. Consistency is important to a brand, but the brand must stay relevant or it will die.

For a business, a brand is perceived through all the points of contact with the firm. It starts with your signage on the front of the building. Is it new looking and accurate? Does it fit your brand's image? I have frequented small businesses that don't have signs at all. I highly recommend that you don't hide from the customer. Does your signage say what your business is and does it invite people in? If not, why not?

Choose your tools and materials wisely, since they also help express your brand. This includes your hardware, software, and even the paper you use for your brochures. Does your equipment communicate your brand as leading edge and current, or are you aligned with the past? Is your voice mail greeting offered by an older mechanical message recorder (with hiss and hum) or is it a new digital system? Is your on-hold music pleasing or is abrasive? Hip-hop may sound too trendy to the folks from the sixties.

Your company name, logo, and tagline must be consistently displayed on all customer-facing material. This includes business cards, letterhead, envelopes, brochures, website, invoices, fax cover sheets, and signage. Color and the mood that it can create help communicate the brand's feel. Fonts need to be consistent across all your marketing communications; choose the font that best fits your image. I recommend being conservative in most cases, since flashy or unusual fonts can be difficult to read and can cause eye fatigue.

The lobby of a building is the first impression (after the signage). Make sure it is clean and comfortable. Does your customer feel at home? Does it smell clean? Does it look professional? Have you posted your mission statement and values statement for your customers to read? Is the furniture new and clean? Does the receptionist look professional and is he or she polite when greeting visitors?

For many businesses, the lobby is now the home page of a website. Does the website help the visitor to solve a problem or get information? It used to be that you had up to four clicks of the mouse to deliver what the website visitor wanted; studies indicate today that it may now be one or two clicks. If that is the case, you better have the right stuff on the home page. See the chapters about websites.

Consider keeping a brand handbook which captures all your branding elements including colors, fonts, phone etiquette, tagline, logo, stationery design, signage graphics, background music, dress code, etc. This can be helpful for communicating your brand's essentials to new employees while emphasizing its importance to existing staff.

Frequently, I am asked how to build a brand in a niche market. As you can see after reading this chapter, branding is a "soft" topic; it is difficult to define and hard to measure. Yet, behind a good brand you usually will find a good company. My answer on how to build a brand is simple; first build a good company that takes responsibility for delivering a unique solution to the target market. Focus your energies on solving the customer problems rather than obsessing about the firm's image. If you establish this special partnership with your customer, your brand will be built. Of course, you need to communicate your branding to your market with consistency and relevancy, but by being uniquely connected to your customer, your brand will be real. It will be believed.

Action: If you have lobby, go sit in it and see how it feels. Are you proud of your lobby?

25. Branding Versus Positioning: What's the Difference?

"Honesty is the best image."

Tom Wilson (1931–) Comic strip creator

OK, here is where the academics start to split hairs over definitions. From my point of view, positioning describes the measurable differences between your solution or product and that of the competitors. It really is a look backwards (i.e., a historical view) based on the evidence gathered by experience or market research. It says what is in your target market's minds. Good positioning is what makes you unique. It is an expression of how your target market describes your firm when compared to your competitors. It is important to understand this is the customers' view, not yours. It is their perception of your firm and how it stacks up to the competition.

Meanwhile, branding is bigger in scope and more ethereal in that it expresses why your customers are loyal or prefer your brand. Maybe less measurable than positioning, but still real, branding is a covenant between the provider and the customer.

That is all you really need to know.

A final comment: You build your brand by creating an image delivered by your logo, tagline, fonts, name, use of color, and sounds: they communicate your ideas, your values, and your personality. Every contact or touch of your customer reinforces the brand.

26. Personal Branding: Be the Brand

"We must become the change we want to see."

Mahatma Gandhi (1869–1948) Indian philosopher and leader

Personal branding, a promise of value for an individual, is the essence of the entrepreneur and will set the tone for the business. From my point of view, corporate brands are personal brands with bigger voices. The firm rallies behind a message that promises value to the target customer.

For the business, the personal brand of the entrepreneur is the foundation of the firm's brand. The supporting cast of employees at the business must emulate the entrepreneur's message. They must share the same vision and values.

To discover your personal brand ask yourself:

- What is your vision?
- How do you stand out?
- What makes you special?
- What is different about you when compared to your peers?
- How are you better?
- What is most important about you?
- What is your secret talent?
- What do people admire most about you?
- What do you aspire to be?

Ask your friends and colleagues about your strengths and your weaknesses. Ask them what is different about you. Analyze their responses. How does it compare with your own assessment?

I recommend that you audit your personal brand. A good exercise is to question everything you do (with your brand in mind) for the next two weeks. Audit your appearance and your phone manners. Carefully review your e-mail and other written correspondence. Are there typos? Is your grammar correct? Do you rely heavily on slang? Are you proud of what you write? How do you handle social encounters? Are you polite and attentive? Take a step back and look at yourself. What are you consciously and unconsciously communicating about yourself, about your brand? How are you dressed? Your living space and your office express your brand. How does it look? What does it say about you and your choices?

The sum of these things makes up your personal brand.

Mark everything you do with your brand. Be consistent. A clever tagline can help communicate your unique value proposition. Use it in all communications. Include it on your business cards, letterhead, and your e-mails. Alternatively, after your e-mail signature add a quotation that is clever or thought provoking.

You can build your personal brand by writing letters to the editor of your local newspaper, or by submitting articles to trade associations. Normally, the editors are starving for something interesting or new, so they will always be available to talk with a new source. Volunteer for speaking opportunities at networking groups, at your local college, or elsewhere in your community. Your involvement with these organizations shouts your brand's message.

What to do next: Add a meaningful quotation to your signature line on your e-mail; choose one that says something consistent with your brand.

27. Public Relations and Publicity

"Ninety-eight percent of the adults in this country are decent, hard-working, honest Americans. The other lousy two percent get all the publicity. But then, we elected them."

Lily Tomlin (1939–) Comic actor

Public relations (also known as PR) is simply defined as any publicity for your product, service, or company that the public thinks is not paid for by you or your company. PR helps establish or maintain good will, while educating the customer about a company, product, or solution.

Most advertising is paid for and is not as believable as PR; most PR is perceived to be more truthful because a third party writes it. The key difference between publicity and advertising is the cost and control. Publicity may be "free", but you cannot control what happens to your message. It can be manipulated, changed, or never sent. A major benefit of advertising is that you can control the message. OK, nothing is free and neither is PR. In fact, if done right, PR is a lot of work. When you see a good piece of PR in an editorial or in a feature story, a lot of hard work went into making that event happen. A PR industry "truism" is that editorial coverage is seven to eight times more valuable as paid advertising.

Examples of PR include getting your name in print with a quote in a local newspaper, being interviewed on the radio since you are an expert on a subject, or being chosen to speak at an industry conference. While these events might have been orchestrated by you or your PR firm, or publicist, you did not buy the time or the space to get your message out. Thus, your words are to be believed.

You can manage your public relations effort by yourself while your firm is small. A grass roots approach to PR can be very effective. A simple tactic is to contact the business editor at your local paper or the specialty publication that focuses on your expertise and let them know that if they ever want to do a story on your field or solution, you are glad to help them. My experience is that these folks are always looking for a story and your call could trigger the next one with your name and opinion featured. Your goal is to establish a relationship with the editor or columnist at the publication; this could be the beginning of a series of many favorable quotes by you in the business section. Make friends with these people and remember it is your job to stay in touch, not theirs.

As your firm grows, hiring a PR agency may become a viable option.

A PR firm has a responsibility to help you define and deliver your message. They also need to help you get to the people who need to hear your message. If the PR firm can't help with the above, then you don't need them. Please be cautious of smaller PR firms since the real base of knowledge and media relationships are usually with the owner and the second-in-command. Make sure that they are actively involved throughout the entire campaign.

Whether you do PR by yourself or hire an agency, you need an evangelist to deliver your firm's message. I feel strongly that it needs to be a single voice to ensure consistency. Your company spokesperson or champion needs to be the "go to" person for the press and media. More often that not, it should be the entrepreneur who does this work and it is not something to delegate. Bigger firms might have the Chief Executive Officer (CEO), the Chief Marketing Officer (CMO), or the even the Chief Technology Officer (CTO) designated for this role. It goes without saying that this person needs to be personable, charismatic, insightful, and above all, a great communicator. The spokesperson needs to be able to think quickly on his or her feet. The role can be very challenging since it is one thing to read a prepared announcement and quite another to react to questions "on the fly" about it. Remember your goal is to influence the opinion of your target audience or the recipient of your message.

Some experts say that body language or nonverbal cues are more important than verbal ones. Statistically in order of importance, body language accounts for 55% of your communication; "para-language" or the use of intonation, pauses, and sighs account for 38%; and the actual verbal content of your message accounts for just 7%. In other words, non-verbal communications can overpower or even contradict, what you say in words. The bottom line: be aware of your body language.

As the chief spokesperson, you need three basic commercials or pitches: the elevator pitch or thirty-second commercial (It used to the sixty-second commercial, but that is just too long in the new millennium.), a ten-minute presentation, and a thirty-minute road show (the long-play version commonly known as "death by PowerPoint").

The elevator pitch is a carefully crafted, memorized statement that says what your firm does; more than a mission statement, this elevator pitch is a sales pitch, albeit a brief one. It should include a problem statement and the customer definition; of course, it should include a description of your solution and the benefits. Frankly, that is a lot to say in thirty seconds, so most people focus on just the benefits. By focusing solely on the benefits, you take away the focus on the customer, which is dead wrong in my opinion. Writing an elevator pitch is hard work and much harder to do than the other two pitches. Consider this pitch as good fodder for cocktail parties when you are asked, "What does your company do?" If people get glazed eyes when you deliver this commercial, it is probably because it is too long.

Often delivered via PowerPoint, this ten-minute presentation is a company overview built around your product or solution. Once again, this is a sales pitch. Although I am not a fan of presentations for selling purposes, this canned pitch may be what the doctor ordered on certain occasions. I will admit that some customers seem to enjoy this type of pain and will actually ask for this type of presentation. (I think that they have just learned to expect them.) Let them eat cake, so to speak.

The thirty-minute road show pitch is tad longer with a product demonstration (if possible) along with handouts. Hopefully, you will get peppered with questions (if not, you did not get the order). My experience is that this long-play version is best suited for investors rather than customers. Investors like to ask pithy questions like "What is your ultimate value proposition?" since they feel compelled to look and sound intelligent. Be prepared to fling a good one back at them, but don't worry since they probably won't listen to your answer anyway.

Whether you do your own PR or hire an agency, the following basic steps are recommended:

- Create the positioning message; what is the one thing that you want your target market to know about you or your firm?
- Write a two- to three-word mantra which describes the message. These will be the words used in your workplace and externally. They must be memorable and believable.
- Your message should be short and memorable for external consumption. Make sure that all employees can echo this message. They need to understand it and believe it along with you and the customer.
- Test your message with your staff, your vendors, and your customers. How does the target audience receive it?
- Adjust your message based on the feedback. Test it again.
- Create press releases (More on that later.) so that you present your pitch in the form of news. More than a commercial, tie the launch of your press releases to a significant event to create timeliness. The press is always interested in what is timely, informative, and they like it to be a bit controversial.
- Create press kits; when they call, you need to send follow-up materials. They always ask for them. This is done by e-mail more and more; some may ask for paper, so have both types ready.
- Create product evaluation kits; these are great selling tools for

customers. Include a sample of your merchandise. This can be done virtually on the web or by mail. Be sure to do it promptly.

- Create mailing lists for customers, prospects, and everyone else that needs to hear your story. This name development is critical and needs to be an ongoing process; the best lists are built by getting permission from visitors to your website. Lists can also be purchased and PR firms can help with this task.
- Introduce yourself to analysts, industry mavens, and people of influence. This may seem daunting on your own, but if you start asking around and watching for names in the industry periodicals, you will find them. This is also when a PR agency helps a lot. Your goal is to build a relationship with these movers and shakers; it is up to you to stay in touch since they won't call you.
- Make some noise! This would be press releases, interviews, and events. Be sure you contact PR Newswire, Business Wire, Market Wire etc. Throw a party! Frequency of contact is the number one criteria in a purchasing decision, so you cannot have enough publicity.
- Track your success by monitoring new leads, number of press quotes, and other indicators of awareness. This will help evaluate the effectiveness of your current PR efforts and help with future PR choices.
- Create a constituency with the readership by seeking feedback and involving them in the critique of your PR effort. Heed their advice and modify what your plan. This will also help facilitate the creation of relationships with the press.

Build awareness, create a constituency, and solve problems; be more than noise. Be a source of knowledge on the problem that your product or solution solves.

To do: Ask your customers what magazines, trade journals, and newspapers they read (online and off-line). Ask what radio stations they listen to and what websites they visit. This is the beginning of your media list.

28. Press Releases Create Publicity By Being Relevant

"I've had a wonderful time, but this wasn't it."

Groucho Marx (1895–1977) Comedian and author

Press releases are written to create publicity and awareness for your firm or your solution; they are also known as PR releases, news releases or press statements. They are not to be confused with "real" news or news articles, which are what the journalists write for the media. The purpose of the press release is to encourage the journalists to write about the contents of the press release; the content of the press release can be almost anything that is relevant or important to the reader. Examples of press release subjects include new product announcements, the creation of a new company, executive management changes, customer wins, partnerships and alliances, trade show product debuts, or a subtle selling document on what is different about your firm or product. Regardless of the content, press releases must be useful, interesting, and accurate.

News wire services are used to broadcast news releases to their online media subscribers, which can include magazines, radio stations, local and national newspapers, television stations, and individual companies. News releases are also mailed, e-mailed, and faxed directly to the media contacts; unfortunately, they get tons of them. Today most recognized web portals and internet sites like Yahoo.com or Google.com will only accept releases from "legitimate" newswire services.

Press releases are written with an angle or bias; the reader knows that the purpose of the press release is to create publicity or garner attention for the firm that issued the press release. The call to action in a press release is to call the press release "contact" for more information, or to create a news article about the content in the press release. Because of this inherent bias by the author of the press release, there is no guarantee that the editor or journalist will respond to the call for action or write an article. To increase the impact of the press release, the content or topic must be timely and relevant to the editor or journalist.

Here are a few tips:

- Be sure to label the press release appropriately; typically, this is done in capital letters at the top of the page (i.e., PRESS

RELEASE). The company contact/s should be listed directly below the press release label. If the press release is urgent or needs immediate attention, indicate that the press release is for immediate release in all capital letters. Otherwise, a release date is posted in all capital letters.

- All press releases need to have a catchy headline to grab the reader's attention, which encourages the reader to continue reading. A sub-headline that clarifies the headline's intent can be a great tool to help keep the attention of the reader.
- The lead paragraph of the news release needs to have "the 5 Ws and the H": who, what, when, where, why, and how. The lead paragraph tells the reader what the press release is about. Keep the first paragraph short; I suggest no more than 30 to 40 words at most.
- The second and third paragraph offer more detail about the topic and often uses quotes to sell the content and to provide a personal touch. A fourth paragraph sums up the release.
- Double-space all press releases and use a simple, easy to read font like Times New Roman or Arial.
- Carefully write your press release by eliminating spelling and grammatical errors. Sloppy press releases will get tossed immediately, since your reader is a professional writer. If you are not a good writer, consider hiring one.
- The press release must be believable and truthful. Good journalists will quickly fact-check your news release for accuracy. Fibs and fluff will be rejected. Avoid bragging and false "build ups". Avoid the use of trite business terms like "state of the art", "unique value proposition", "revolutionary", "ground-breaking", "paradigm shift", and "breakthrough technological advances" since the editors will just filter this jargon out or simply disregard the press release.
- Short and concise press releases are best since the media contacts receive dozens of press releases daily. One to two pages will suffice. Write them in a business tone and never use personal pronouns like I or we (except in quotes).
- Consider segmenting your PR audience by sub-segment or by cohort. A general press release blasted to thousands who don't care about your message is a waste of time. If possible, modify your message to each of the different segments; this creates relevancy and increases the impact of the PR effort.
- Press releases are relevant by being timely; you need to communicate why your press release is news today. Try to tie your con-

tent to a special event coming up; yesterday's news is not worth printing.

- Remember that the editor or journalist who reads your press release is looking for content that will be interesting, important, or relevant for his readers. He does not care if people go to your website or if you sell anything. Write the press release to help the journalist accomplish his objectives.
- Consider building a pitch to go with the release and "embargo-ing" the release to give your favorite journalists time to consider the release before the official distribution date of the press release. This delay gives you time to pitch the journalists with the possibility of a briefing (a multi-party conference call or one-on-one phone conversation) to add value to the story and increase the chance that the story will be printed. Your favorite journalists will appreciate the "scoop" (i.e., the first shot at the story).
- Seek feedback on your press releases; listen carefully and tweak your future press releases to make them more relevant.

One more thing: Editors and journalists are people. Reach out to them by phone to introduce yourself ahead of time. Let them know of your desire to help. When they need you, they might just choose to call you, instead of someone else.

29. Cause Marketing; Do Good and Get Rewarded For It

"We make a living by what we get, but we make a life by what we give."

Winston Churchill (1874–1965) British leader

Giving time to a charitable event or organization can create a strong promotional event for yourself, build your network, and help build your brand. "Cause marketing", as it is often called, is a marketing activity that supports a charitable event, a cause, or a non-profit organization. Although philanthropy by corporations has been a common promotional tool for a long time, connecting this good work with a companies advertising and public relations campaign is relatively new.

Some think that American Express may have been the innovator of "modern" cause marketing with their 1983 campaign for the Statue of Liberty. In an effort to promote the image of American Express as a patriotic and responsible American business, they publicly agreed to donate a penny to the restoration of the Statue of Liberty with each credit card transaction (or traveler's check). This campaign went on for about six months and contributed millions of dollars to the charity. The publicity and goodwill that American Express received in exchange for this good deed was unprecedented. At the time, this was headline news in the Wall Street Journal, the New York Times, and on television news. Better yet, according to Daniel Gross in his book, SHARED ASSETS, American Express increased new credit card applications by 45%, while existing card usage went up 28%. Essentially, the campaign gave consumers a reason to choose American Express over other credit cards

Think of cause marketing as philanthropy with a business purpose; this technique can be used by small businesses, too. While doing something good for the community or for a favorite cause, you can create great publicity for yourself and your firm. My experience is that you will make the most of this type of opportunity by jumping in with both feet and by being actively involved as a leader in the charitable event's planning process. Gaining access to new relationships may be the biggest reward. Devote the time to get to know the others involved in the charity; you can build relationships that might pay off later. Position yourself as a leader and evangelist for the cause.

A key element in cause marketing is sincerity. Your support must be genuine, which will allow your energy to show through. This will attract others with similar motivations. Others will see or feel your commitment and they will know that you are genuine. This state of mind is tantalizing to others and fun. Be genuine and others will join you.

Non-profit organizations such as Junior Achievement need the support and mentoring from leaders in the business community. I have served on numerous community and non-profit boards like Southern California Junior Achievement and have met some extraordinary people who became my friends and trusted advisors. Most of these people volunteered because they wanted to give back to the community while expanding their personal networks.

Additionally, I have discovered that this type of work leads to other like opportunities with other non-profit organizations. Often the board members of one organization, who are active in other non-profit boards, will recommend board members for other boards. Surprisingly, the philanthropic "insiders" who do this good work is often a small circle of powerful people with good intentions; if you are inside that circle, you have access to many powerful connections for future business.

The publicity garnered from this "good work" can be extraordinary including interviews on behalf of the organization with the local and national press, television and radio. This philanthropic work creates access to business leaders, politicians, and other like-minded executives. These relationships are priceless and so is the publicity you get for giving back to community; you cannot buy this type of recognition. You earn it.

Getting started: What charity means the most to you? Call them up and see if you can help. You might surprise them, since they are used to making calls for help.

30. Throw a Party When Something Significant Happens

"Small opportunities are often the beginning of great enterprises."

Demosthenes (384–322 B.C.) Greek orator & politician

Ken Kragen, sports and celebrity agent, wrote in his book LIFE IS A CONTACT SPORT about strategically managing events in your career and at your business; he said, "Concentrating on three or more major events within a short period of time will set the stage for a major breakthrough". He feels that to get from one plateau to another requires a series of events in a short period. He thinks stars are made rather than born.

Companies and their brands can be propelled to the next level by managing a single significant occurrence. When something happens that is unique, dramatic, or sensational for a product, a person, or a company, you could have a tremendous public relations opportunity. Sometimes these occurrences happen without any notice, while others are planned well in advance. An example of an unplanned occurrence would be if you helped at the scene of an accident and, because of your efforts, a life was saved. If you were an off-duty fireman, this would be a tremendous PR event for the fire department. The local papers would eat it up. An example of a planned occurrence would be having your firm considered in a "Small Business of the Year" event (which you have to apply and present a justification for), sponsored by the local Chamber of the Commerce. If named the Small Business of the Year, this could be a PR opportunity for many months or years after the award.

For the entrepreneur, significant occurrences do happen and can be made more significant with an event strategy. A significant happening like this must be real and tangible. It cannot be forged or made up. Like the story that is remembered, a significant occurrence lives on in your customers' minds. You can make the most of a significant occurrence, whether it is a product launch, a store opening, or another major event, by strategically promoting it. The occurrence can be self-created or it can be organic, but it needs to be promoted by you. It cannot promote itself.

Let's say that your company has a breakthrough technology that will save your customers money and time; your new products will apply this technology, while your competitors cannot even come close. Turn this new product rollout into a PR extravaganza by coordinating all aspects of promotion and publicity.

The plan would go something like this:

- Create a message or mantra which is a simple sentence or phrase that describes the occurrence and the technology announcement; make it fun or catchy, since you want everyone to remember it.
- Display the message everywhere: on business cards, stickers, flyers, trinkets, billboards, banner ads on the web, etc.
- Announce the new technology at a major trade show or conference; remember to bring brochures, press releases, and "tchotchkes" to commemorate the event.
- Hand out a white paper (a detailed description on the technology) at the announcement; put the white paper on your website.
- Time the announcement so it shines by itself and won't compete with other events. Don't announce a new recipe for rabbit stew on Easter Sunday.
- Tell the trade press about this announcement; reach out to the appropriate editors. Press releases are the normal stock in trade and a good thing, but I would also call your media contacts directly.
- Send out a press release to all other pertinent media sources, customers, and prospects.
- Have your website updated along with your brochure materials; testimonials would help and they should tie back to the benefits of your product.
- Hold an open house at your facility inviting key industry figures; make it a big party.
- Have your employees talk it up with all customers; create an initiative to tell every customer that they talk with about this news.
- Advise your financial network of this occurrence; this may help reaffirm why they invested in your business and why they might invest again.
- Tell all of your suppliers about this breakthrough; they love to gossip, so give them something good.
- Train your sales force to sell this new technology.
- Do a coordinated telephone, e-mail, and mail campaign the same day as the announcement to let everyone know about the great news!

Opportunities like this don't come often, so when they do you need to make the most of them. This is not a time to be timid or careful. Rather, this the time to be bold, proud, and boastful. This is your time to shine. Everybody loves a winner.

One last thought: Although some major occurrences just happen, we know about most of them well in advance. What do you anticipate will be your biggest event next year? Create a plan to promote it.

31. Viral Marketing is Contagious

"Word of mouth is the best medium of all."

William Bernbach (1911–1982) Businessman

Viral marketing is a trendy name for innovative publicity-generating techniques at play in the market place. Broadly defined this could include unconventional methods of advertising and promotion; most often viral marketing is thought of as internet based in the B2C (business-to-consumer) market.

Viral marketing uses existing social networks such as personal e-mail lists or company directories to spread brand awareness, ideas, or buzz. The process is grass roots propelled much like an epidemic with one person infecting the next. All this happens in fast succession. Tools of the viral marketing trade can include e-mails, e-mails with attachments, and blogs. Instant messaging (IM) and cell phones are new turf for viral marketing; these channels of distribution favor the younger crowd who are more likely to use IM and text messaging. They also may be more likely to accept messages without regard for viruses or privacy issues.

I suppose the crudest form of viral marketing is a chain letter in the form of an e-mail (Yes, in the old days we actually got letters beseeching us not to break the chain.) which requests that the reader pass it along to a friend or, better yet, to a whole list of friends.

Sometimes the instigator of a viral marketing campaign hides the message in the content and finally discloses the message or brand at the end of the video or e-mail. The goal in this case is just advertising. Television advertisements have also adopted this "hide the ball" technique. For example, ever watch a commercial and ask yourself, "What is this commercial about?" The goal is to hook you into watching the whole ad to increase the likelihood that you will remember it.

The most important element in a viral marketing campaign is the content itself; the content must be funny, compelling, unusual, useful, shocking, or just plain stupid. Always included or buried in the content is the sponsor's brand or message. The recipient is entertained or inspired by the content and then chooses to pass it on to the next friend or contact. This is often referred to as "word-of-mouth marketing". It goes on from there.

Thus, this approach is a real-world demonstration of reference accounts gone wild: advertising that is recommended by a friend or colleague. This method propels the message with speed, it's cheap or no cost, and it pinpoints your customer perfectly. The downside is a lack of control you have of who actually gets the message. In addition, you have no real ability to track what happens.

Small businesses can get viral by creating simple e-mails in the form of forwarded jokes, quizzes, and photos. Video clips are common but beware the videos that take too long to load by the average PC user. Maybe the best viral technique for a small firm is to encourage your e-mail list to forward your newsletter to their own e-mail lists. When the new visitors visit your site, you can register them. Tell a friend!

More actions: Visit some of your favorite websites and give permission to receive their e-mail newsletters. Review them for content and format; they might have great ideas for your next e-mail newsletter.

32. Buzz!

"Eighty percent of success is showing up"

Woody Allen (1935–) Comedian, author, and director

Generally associated with the internet, buzz is a type of PR that reflects an excitement about your firm. The feeling is that you are onto something big or new, maybe it is the next big thing. It is like you have won the race before it even started. I have witnessed this buzz with software products, where being first was more important than having a product that worked effectively. (The software maker ironically thought that they could debug the product later.) You may have witnessed this crazy herd behavior during the dotcom era when new products (bugs and all) were launched before they were ready. All this was accepted as cool. To a degree, this mindset continues; buyers beware.

So, what does the buzz sound or look like? I guess you know it when you hear it or read about it. Typically, the "next big thing" is profiled by an industry analyst and declared the best new thing ever. For legitimate reasons or because of pure momentum, the press grabs the story and pumps the firm or product. The fever pitch grows. Next, the decision makers hear about it and tell their friends about it. Again, it goes on.

You can create a buzz, too. If you have a truly innovative product or solution, you need to get to the innovators and early adopters. Don't bother selling to the late majority or laggards, they won't buy unless they have to buy and even then, they will fight it. This is much harder than it sounds, since as entrepreneurs we naturally believe everyone will want our product. In practice, most buyers make safe decisions and won't stick their neck out for something new or untested.

Let's explore this some more. DIFFUSIONS OF INNOVATIONS, a seminal book written by Everett Rogers in the early sixties, introduced the thinking that different sociological groups adopt innovation at different rates. He grouped adopters of innovation or change into subgroups with common traits or characteristics.

The categories are:

- Innovators—educated, adventuresome, risk takers, daring
- Early Adopters—social leaders, educated, trend setters, status seekers
- Early Majority—followers who wait for the cue to buy by the mass media

- Late Majority—traditional, sometimes skeptical, lower socio-economic status
- Laggards—fearful, look for insight from neighbors and friends

Simply stated, innovators are the first to buy innovative products or solutions; they thrive on being first and are almost reckless in their desire to have the latest thing. For example, they were the first to have HDTV in the home, long before sufficient programming existed to truly justify the purchase. This was a very small group of buyers. Early adopters followed soon after. They take their lead from the innovators, but they buy innovative products more for status and utility. One good thing about innovators and early adopters is that they leave tracks. They buy certain types of magazines, belong to unique associations, visit certain websites, and are frequently referred to or quoted since they love to be on the "bleeding edge".

The larger groups follow with the early majority embracing change when it is popular or common. They take the lead from the early adopters and are price sensitive. Next in line are the late adopters who are very price sensitive and will buy innovations only when it is a part of mass culture. They may wait until peer pressure forces them. Laggards won't buy innovative products unless necessity or the government forces them to.

Many innovative firms waste time and money trying to sell to the early majority, late majority, and laggards. Don't waste your time since these people may only buy a new and better solution if they are forced to do so. The streets are paved with failed business plans that describe huge markets for innovative solutions based on the thinking that all customers will want to buy the next new thing.

Food for thought: Are you an innovator, early adopter, early majority, late majority, or laggard? Why?

33. Radio Can Create Instant Awareness for Your Firm

"Radio is the theater of the mind; television is the theater
of the mindless."

Steve Allen (1921–2000) Comedian and talk show host

Radio can be a terrific way to position yourself as a "knowledge broker" while promoting your business. Talk radio may be the best radio format for an interview along with the news segments on traditional radio stations. Getting interviewed on a radio program is not as tricky as you might think. Radio station managers are always looking for interesting topics and guests; like you in your business, they trying to be different from the competition. The challenge is to get on their radar, so to speak. Before approaching them, study the station's target audience. Who is their customer? What demographic are they targeting? This may help alter your story or pitch.

Here are a few ideas on improving your odds at getting on the air and some tips on making the most of your opportunity, once you get it:

- Go to the radio station website and you will find information about the station's mission, the audience that they serve, and what content they cover. Make yourself knowledgeable of what they are trying to do.
- They sometimes archive previously-aired material on the website which should give you a feel for their content or message.
- Like any company, there are numerous points of contact including the on-air personalities, the program managers, the PR department, or the producers. You can contact these folks directly, but don't expect a call back until they need you. Getting referred in is best, but that works only if you know someone who knows them.
- You may find a link the on the website that gives instructions on how to contact the station by e-mail. This is the formal channel communication into the radio station. They are expecting people to contact them; unfortunately, they generally screen out 90% of the requests. The good news is that the radio staff is always on the hunt for news, feature stories or talent. That is you.

- As simple as it sounds, listening to the radio station will probably give you the best sense of what the station is all about.
- Maintain a dialog with radio stations via press releases. Note that turnover in radio staff is notoriously high and it will take great effort to keep your database current. Both e-mail and direct mail can do the trick. People get fired a lot in radio, so don't get too attached to them.
- When they need an "expert", it is typically because of a "hot" news story. This means that they have little time to go looking for you so it helps to be in their database as a "knowledge broker". When they need you, you will have to drop everything to help them or they will just contact someone else on their list.
- I recommend contacting the show producers along with the on-air personalities to let them know of your special knowledge. Your timing will never be right when you approach them, so you need to express your interest and ongoing availability.
- Radio stations are required by the FCC to make public service announcements (also known as PSAs in the trade). Your knowledge or message may fit the station's criteria for a PSA. Often the PR department will have the job to find PSA material. They can help you contact the right person to speak with at the station.
- The straight news at the radio station is typically traffic, crime, and weather. They will be quick to admit that it is very boring, repetitive stuff. Because of that, they are always on the hunt for feature or human-interest stories. It could be that your business and "knowledge" fit the bill.
- As a guest, the good news is that you are an expert and, therefore, you know more than the interviewer and more than the audience (generally speaking). So, relax and speak as if talking to a friend. Keep your responses concise, but colorful. Visualize the audience listening to you and smiling at your comments. Be prepared to answer the same question several times during the interview, radio personalities are surprisingly poor interviewers and worse listeners.
- If the interview is on the phone, close the door to your office and let everyone know that you are on the radio. No interruptions allowed. Always use a landline phone since cordless phones and cell phones just don't sound right. Can you say dropped call?
- An interview at the radio station requires that you dress professionally, (i.e., look the part) although radio personnel tend to be a casual group themselves.

- When you are done offer your contact information. This way people know how to contact you for follow-up questions. Often the station will allow you to release your website address over the air.
- If the station records the segment, ask for a copy. You can include this on your website. After the fact, you can promote the recorded interview via e-mail to your website's registered guests.
- Be sure to follow up with thank you cards to the station. Send a card to everyone that you met. Express your willingness to do this again.
- Do your best to establish a relationship with the on-air talent and the producers; if they like you, they will invite you back.

Action: Ask your customers what radio stations are programmed on their car radios; this should help you figure out what radio stations to target.

34. *What's the Difference between an Advertising Agency and a Public Relations Firm?*

"The lion and the calf shall lie down together, but the calf won't get much sleep"

Woody Allen (1935–) Comedian, author, and director

The lines are blurring, but advertising agencies and public relations firms are in different businesses, although the end goal is the same. They hope to help you sell more and they want to take credit for it, if that happens.

The advertising agency manages marketing communications for the contracting firm or client. The agency can vary in size from a handful of professionals to a thousand-person firm. Agencies normally generate fees or commissions by taking a percentage of the media purchases made by the client firm. The large agencies or full service agencies will provide creative services, access to the media, production, and account management. Essentially, the full-service advertising agency is a marketing consultant that will function as a member of the client's marketing staff to help create, produce, purchase, and manage all advertising from strategy to concept to delivery. One more thing, the message that is delivered in an advertising campaign is paid for by the client and everyone knows that.

Public relation firms (also known as PR firms) function to convince the media to get the client's message out; in this case, the message is positioned to be news rather than advertising. This is called publicity. The expertise at the PR firm is their intimacy with and access to media contacts and to the gurus in the industry, who can help the client get noticed. PR firms can help you create your message, pitch articles to the media, help with market research, and prepare speeches.

The confusion about the difference between an advertising agency and a PR firm comes from the fact that these two entities are combining forces due to economic pressures. Add to this the general decline in the effectiveness of traditional advertising. Many large advertising firms offer PR services or have an affiliate company that does. Consolidation has also entered the picture because the bigger an ad agency is, the bigger their purchasing power with the media.

For a small business, choosing the ad agency and the PR firm is a decision for the future; while the firm is small, you can do much this work by yourself. When the time comes, I recommend you consider the following factors in your advertising and PR firm selection process:

- Consider selecting ad agencies and PR firms that specialize in your industry. Choose ad agencies and PR firms that understand your business and actually care about what you do.
- Start by working on a project-by-project basis; start small at the beginning. It is OK to change firms and shop. They won't like this and will advise against, by the way.
- Agree on a set of metrics with both PR firms and ad agencies to measure success; for advertising, it could be the number of impressions or sales leads. For PR firms it could be the number of published quotes or inches of publicity in print.
- Depending on your size and need, consider doing these activities in-house with a dedicated employee who has advertising or PR experience.
- Proximity can be a real issue if you will need to work with them frequently; find firms that are close by. Your time is valuable; so don't waste it on the road.
- Verify the experience of the firm's management team; pedigree counts.
- Cost is a factor and this type of support is not cheap. Consider at least three firms before you go forward.
- If you have media contacts, ask who they might recommend for advertising and PR support. It is likely that they will be familiar and very opinionated about who you might choose.
- Avoid conflicts of interest with ad agencies and PR firms who work with competitors.

Action: Start collecting advertisements that catch your eye and entice you to read them; keep a file folder on your PC and in your desk for future reference.

35. Advertising's Dirty Little Secret

"Half the money I spend on advertising is wasted; the trouble is
I don't know which half."

George Santayana (1863–1952) Philosopher

Advertising is a waste of money for most entrepreneurial firms since advertising is often ineffective. Traditional print advertising is generally wasted money since gazillions of impressions sent to the gazillions of the wrong people does no one any good, except for the people who designed, printed, or distributed the advertisement. Radio and TV can be expensive, although satellite and cable offer some interesting options to target the customer. Still they throw out a big net with few fish caught.

People don't believe it anyway. Consumers are bombarded with advertising every day. It is estimated that consumers are exposed to 3,000 advertisements a day and we are numb from it all. Ironically, consumers understand that advertising is paid for and not to be believed. So why do firms waste money on advertising? I think it is as simple as we have been taught to do this by the advertising firms. Whoops.

We are witnessing the decline and ultimate death of traditional advertising, which has existed for many years as a steady-stream dialog of messages that say, "Buy this today." Inundated with too many messages, the consumer cannot remember the messages nor can the consumer tell them apart. Few advertisements are memorable and those that are may be memorable for the wrong reasons such as shock value, vulgarity, sexual innuendo, or mindless repetition (my favorite).

Managing the advertising budget in the new millennium is increasingly difficult to do. The traditional methods that have worked for many years now seem to have less cachet, or may not work at all. Advertising on network television and radio has long been a mainstay for the advertising industry along with print advertising in newspapers and magazines. Enter the internet age and we find the rules have all changed. It seems that technology has changed everything. TiVo eliminates television commercials. People read fewer newspapers and spend increasingly more time on the internet. Printed yellow pages look to be tomorrow's dinosaur. New advertising vehicles with great possibilities have landed on the scene including things like podcasting, blogging, wikis, viral marketing, and "advergaming" (the placement of games in advertising or vice versa). Finally, search engine marketing has become a bigger and more powerful tool as entrepreneurs turn to the internet to find the customer.

For the small business, advertising is often ineffective because it is not tested before the money is spent; often the entrepreneur feels obligated to advertise and simply does it because that is what one does. A partial remedy is to always test your advertising before spending the coin. Focus groups can smoke out issues before you launch a campaign; the issues can be tested quantitatively with e-mail surveys. It is better to spend a little money on research first to avoid a wasted advertising campaign.

Beyond that, track all advertising expenditures, track all responses, and track all sales related to those responses. This will help you determine the merit of the advertising investment; it may really scare you. The lack of direct feedback or real sales leads will be modest at best.

Advertising works the best when the reader or listener thinks the advertisement was written just for him or her. As a niche marketer you know and understand the special needs of your target audience; make sure your advertising reflects this knowledge. This is achieved by a very personal message to your target audience. I recommend that you write your ads for people, not end-users, or market segments. Visualize the reader or listener as they encounter the advertising message. How will they feel? How will they respond?

Additionally, a positive message is overwhelmingly preferred to a negative message. Ironically, many advertisements are negative. Think of the last political advertisement that you saw on TV. Most are negative and turn off the viewer.

Your action: Write a paragraph about what you want your customers to know about your firm or product. Use no more than thirty words.

36. Advertising Outdoors and Other Great Places

"Outside of a dog, a book is a man's best friend and inside of a dog,
it is too dark to read."

Groucho Marx (1890–1977) Comedian and author

Depending on your business, there are many other ways and other places to advertise. Consider going outdoors!

Outdoor advertising includes bus and automobile signage, billboards, buses, and trains, benches, sides of buildings, kiosks, and even bumper stickers. In addition, don't forget the sign on the outside of your building, if you have one. Outdoor advertising messages must be very concise and attention getting. While you need to stay consistent with your branding, bright colors are recommended. The person who reads your sign typically only has a few seconds to read and comprehend the message. The first purpose of the sign is branding followed by a call to action, which could include going to a website or calling a phone number.

For businesses with a fleet of vehicles, placing signage on the door or side of the vehicle is a great way to communicate with prospects. The outstanding benefit of this advertising method is that it is "perfectly placed" right in front of your prospect, since your company vehicle is most often servicing customers where the customers live or work. For firms that have drivers who use their own automobiles, inexpensive magnetic signs can be used which adhere to the car door. Window-held, rooftop signs work well, with the most common example being pizza delivery. If your business has a large delivery truck, it makes good sense to place signage on it. When the truck is not in use, park the vehicle where people can see it.

Billboards work best when they are placed near your business. They can be very expensive, but can be very effective at delivering a repetitive message to a prospect. Bus and train benches can also promote your brand like billboards do, but at a more affordable rate. A weakness to this approach is that sometimes people sit on your message, so to speak. Auto traffic and pedestrians can block the view.

Although I find it personally very annoying, advertising at movie theaters is one of the newer locations for getting your message out. This can be particularly effective with a local audience for a carpet cleaner or a restaurant. Before the movie starts, the average theater patron could see your message three to six times. It is very low cost.

It is also possible to partner with other businesses, which target the same customer as your business. I had a client that manufactured fine-quality entertainment centers; he partnered with the local big screen television retailer who agreed to display the entertainment centers on the big-screen TV showroom floor. The TV retailer did not carry entertainment centers, but was commonly asked questions about how to fit the TVs with entertainment centers. This "furniture discussion" was so important to the prospective buyer that the buyer would often pick out a big-screen TV but would hesitate to buy the TV until the entertainment center decision or research was resolved. By partnering together, both companies got what they wanted. More often than not, the entertainment center maker got a referral and the TV retailer got a TV sale.

Advertising in unusual places can also reap benefits. Recently, I went through Los Angeles International airport security and had to remove my shoes, coat, and other terrorist attire. (I am only joking!) I reached for a plastic tub to put my belongings into and discovered that at the bottom of the tub was an advertisement for a major office supplies store. It gave me a good chuckle.

This weekend: Go to a movie and count the number of ads you see before the movie starts.

37. Still Using the Yellow Pages?

"If you don't find it in the index, look very carefully through
the entire catalogue."

Sears, Roebuck, and Company Consumer's Guide, 1897

If you are still devoting significant dollars to the yellow pages, you might want to reconsider your budget. The printed yellow page books are definitely on the way out.

The younger buyer first looks to Google, Yahoo!, or MSN search engines on the internet even when looking to buy local services. Having grown up with laptops, this is just second nature to them since they are "native PC users". The internet allows buyers to comparison shop easily and faster. The advent of the internet on cell phones and smart phones is opening up a whole new arena for search.

The older buyer may still go the yellow pages, as will other demographic groups that are slow to do business on the internet. Lower income and minority groups may also lag behind the younger buyer; the printed yellow pages may be fine for them now, but not for long.

A good use of your advertising dollar would be to make sure that your business is included in search engine databases. Even if you don't have a website, make sure you are listed on the appropriate web directories; list your business name, services offered, 800 number, address, etc.

I do recommend that you have a website, since most people doing a search will want to next visit your website after they have identified your firm in a search. You might want to do a search on yourself or your company. See if you can find yourself. If you don't turn up in the first two pages of text search data, you are in trouble; most web searchers won't go to the third page. See the chapter on getting listed in Google, Yahoo!, and MSN.

If you want to use the yellow pages most effectively, plan on spending significant money. Research studies have shown that bigger ads get more calls. Check and see what size ad your direct competitors use and then jump up to the next size or larger. Also, like in all print advertising, color demands attention and will help your ad response rate. If you are a local business, be sure to emphasize your location. Many buyers prefer to work with a local business. I am personally drawn to an advertisement that portrays the business as "owner operated"; I like doing business with small firms that have a pride of ownership. Be sure to include your website address in the advertisement.

Things are changing. The decades-long tradition of the printed yellow pages is dying. Decrease your spending in this category now and move the budget dollars to other advertising and promotional categories such as your website.

Things to do: Review the yellow-page advertising for your industry; look for clever advertising ideas such catch phrases, graphics, promotions, etc.

38. If You Advertise, Be Sure to Measure It

"There's a fine line between fishing and just standing
on the shore like an idiot."

Steven Wright (1955–) Comedian

Advertising is tough for most small businesses since it is expensive, difficult to connect with your target customer, and hard to measure for effectiveness. However, there some tricks when setting up your advertising campaign to ensure that the campaign's effectiveness can be measured. The simplest method for tracking advertising is to ask the customer how they heard about your business or product. Most of the time, your customers will tell you exactly how they found you; this could be because of advertising or not.

If your campaign requires or allows them to call in on the phone, set up a separate phone number. When that new line rings, you obviously know that the advertisement created the opportunity. If this is a large-scale campaign that has different customer segments or different advertising mediums involved, you can create multiple phone numbers for tracking purposes. For example, if the scale of your campaign is large enough and you are using multiple magazines as your advertising vehicle, you could set up separate phone numbers for each magazine. This tracking data could prove powerful when choosing which magazine to use for your next campaign.

Another trick for tracking the incoming calls is to have your customer call requesting different names or aliases; in this case, the customer calls asking for a specific individual to hear more about the special offer. When the phone rings and the customer wants to speak with "Bob," you know that the caller saw your ad in FIELD AND STREAM (not GOOD HOUSEKEEPING).

Coupons or special pricing can also be keyed to separate advertising methods. On a postcard mailing that has a mail-in tear off, the tear off can be color coded or marked to indicate which magazine worked. Separate mail addresses can be effective for advertising campaign tracking efforts; add a P.O. Box for the campaign. The same technique works on the web; set up separate sites for each campaign. Or, on your website, have them indicate how they found your website when they fill out the permission documents.

Most of these suggestions are inexpensive and simple to implement for tracking advertising. The data should be helpful when making choices about your next advertising campaign.

One more thing: Add up all the money you have spent on advertising in the last three years. Create a list of all the customers that said they found you because of the ad. Calculate the cost per lead. This can very scary.

39. *Your Name Here*

"A good name is better than riches."

Miguel Cervantes (1547–1616) Novelist and playwright

Naming your business, along with your product or solution, is a huge decision and one that you should research thoroughly, choose carefully, and test with your target market. Here are a few ideas on what to consider:

- The shorter, the better. Shorter names are more memorable, easier to type into Google, and more flexible since longer names tend to be more specific, if not more limiting.
- Include a solution in the title. For example, the Ford "Mustang" infers that it will be a fast or exciting car. It communicates reckless abandon, which appeals to the risk taker in some of us. The image of the Mustang also means beauty to some and power to others. It is timeless.
- Make sure that you can expand the title to other products, other geographies, and services. Like a shorter name, a more generic name allows you to offer new solutions, which might have not been in your original marketing plan. The name "Google" seems to have no limitations, although I doubt that I would name my firm Google. A better example would be the name for an automobile repair shop; it might be better to name it "Earl's Garage" instead of "Earl's Tune Ups". The word garage allows you to do auto bodywork and transmissions if you decide to expand your line of services. "Earl's Tune Ups" is very limiting.
- Avoid trends or fads since your business or product might have a long life. The Mustang is timeless; the image is just as effective today as it was in 1964 when Ford introduced this moniker. A bad example from a few years back might be a music store named "Mike's Laser Disc Store". Who would have guessed that laser discs would have such a short product life? "Mike's Music" would have been a safer, albeit boring choice.
- Use an original expression, which is unique to the product or firm. Avoid the use of clichés since we have all heard them before. Instead, choose a name that stands out and demands attention. "Dunkin' Donuts" is a far better name than "Tom's Donuts".

- Include benefits of the solution in the name, if possible. This can be achieved by an image created by the choice of words used or an invented name. For example, combining the Latin word for truth, "veritas", with the word "horizon", created "Verizon Wireless". Combined they create an image of constancy, integrity, and no limits (at least, that is what their ad agency told them).
- Your name can be outrageous or daring, since your objective is to get noticed, while informing your customer about what you do. "DreamWorks", the brainchild of Steven Spielberg, develops, produces, and distributes films, video games, and television programming.
- Don't offend by accidentally referencing race, gender, ethnicity, heritage, etc. Marketplace diversity requires you to think about how the name will be interpreted by people different from yourself.
- Business names need to tie to domain name. This is getting harder and harder to do with the proliferation of existing domain names. In particular, if you want a domain name that ends in ".com", the preferred choice for businesses, you will be challenged to create something new or you will have to use multiple words.

You should know: Many books that don't sell well get new titles. Sometimes, this is all it takes to make a best seller. Do you need to rename your business?

40. Taglines Help People Remember You

"Nothing happens unless first a dream."

Carl Sandburg (1878–1967) Poet

A short phrase following a logo or company name may prove to be the most powerful words you will ever write about your small business. Good taglines are memorable. Remember these? Some these are decades old and still part of our culture:

- "Just do it" by Nike
- "Melts in Your Mouth, Not in Your Hands" for M&Ms Candy by Mars
- "Where America Shops" by Sears
- "You Deserve a Break Today" by McDonald's
- "We Try Harder" by Avis
- "Breakfast of Champions" for Wheaties Cereal by General Mills
- "Got Milk?" by the California Milk Board
- "Fly the Friendly Skies" by United Airlines

Writing good taglines is challenging, but you don't need a consultant to do it for you. Here are some basics:

- Figure out what your message is about. What do you want people to remember about your product or service? Who are your customers?
- Review your mission statement and values statement. What jumps off the page most? What words are most important? Mix them up into different combinations.
- Evaluate other taglines from other firms and other industries. Which do you like? Why?
- Look for other taglines in everyday life. You will find them everywhere. Write them down. Billboards often have great taglines. Take notice.
- Write down words that fit your product or service.
- Go the thesaurus and look for other like words.
- Include a benefit in the tagline if you can. For example, the

tagline "Breakfast of Champions" tells you that if you eat Wheaties, you will be a champion.

- Include the customer in the tagline. For example, the tagline "You Deserve a Break Today" is about "you" the customer.
- One idea is to manipulate a cliché or popular phrase and to make it uniquely yours. For example, I read a headline of an article out of the American Airlines magazine AMERICAN WAY written by Jim Shahin that read, "The geek shall inherit the earth." Obviously, a takeoff on the biblical phrase "The meek shall inherit the earth". What a great tagline that would be for a computer repair shop!
- Start writing short phrases or sentences that deliver your message.
- Rank your ideas and try to simplify them as much as possible.
- Remember short taglines are the most memorable. Seldom are they longer than three or four words.
- Taglines should be written in plain English, be pronounceable, and be easily spelled.
- Give some thought to creating a tagline that will tie to your domain name on the internet. If you do this, it will give you a powerful marketing tool. Note the domain name "breakfastofchampions.com" is owned by General Mills.
- Beware of double meanings or nuances that could offend some. Be politically correct.
- Pick your best three taglines and test them with your staff, customers, and vendors. The results might surprise you. Remember it is not about what you think. It is what others think.
- Adjust the taglines with their feedback and test them again. Choose the best.
- Start over if the taglines are not working since a good tagline could outlive you.
- You might go back and test with a large group. I would look for an approval rating of 75% or better.

The best taglines appear near the logo and should be proudly displayed on business cards, letterhead, brochures, uniforms, signage, invoices, and your website.

While you have a minute: Make a list of the words or phrases that best describe your firm's essence.

41. So What Does a Good Logo Look Like?

"People see our logo, and think we are blood-drinking devil worshippers, which we are, of course."

Adrian Smith (1957–) From Iron Maiden, the heavy metal rock band

You know a good logo when you see one. It somehow gets your attention and makes you think or pause. It communicates a message or an essence. It describes the brand. It tells a story about your firm's identity. Or, at least it should.

If you have big bucks, hire a logo consultant. Most logo consultants or designers will want to get to know your brand before they can start. Since you want them to truly understand you and your company, I would disclose your mission, your values, your long-term goals, and arrange for a happy customer to speak with the designer. It is time well spent. Often the designer will start with the company name in text form and display it in various fonts. The designer will "play" with the letters and look. From that exercise, shapes can develop and the creative process continues.

As far as shape is concerned, know that smooth lines or rounded edges can convey serene or passive messages, while jagged edges or sharp corners communicate urgency or aggression. The shape needs to be balanced and simple. Also, size matters. Consider how a logo will look on a business card; if it works on small scale, it will likely look OK when blown up on the web or on a brochure. Also, make sure the logo can be faxed clearly; overly ornate logos lose detail when faxed, while some are not even readable.

Color is an interesting subject and one hotly debated amongst my designer friends. Colors evoke mood and can be provocative or benign. When choosing a color, you should consider the colors supported by web browsers; it turns out there are 216 colors on the web palette. Ever notice that many of most memorable logos are invariably red and/or yellow? It is no accident, since red and yellow are attention grabbing and sometimes irritating colors. Think of the most successful companies and look at the logos: Coca Cola, Nike, and McDonald's. So should your firm have a red or yellow logo? Yes, if that color reflects the image of your firm and if you need a logo that screams, "Look at me". Otherwise, there are many other colors on the color wheel to choose. Orange is a hot color for technology companies as is bright green; I am told these are very "retro".

Since most logos are long lived, I am inclined to vote for conservative logo color, shape, and feel. But how I feel or what I think about your logo is far less important than how others perceive your logo. I recommend that you test your logo with your staff, vendors, and customers. It seems that everyone has an opinion on logos. It best to provide choices to your test group and let them choose among options; be thick-skinned for this exercise since the feedback can be brutal.

An important objective for a good logo is for it to be legible and understood. If you have ever examined a logo and not really understood what it was or what the image was trying to say, then you have seen a bad logo. Logos must very quickly communicate and be understood. Intricate or arcane logos will fail to meet this objective. Also, when testing prospective logos, make sure that you don't offend your potential audience due to accidental ethnic or racial slurs, gender bias, or other such blunders.

Your logo style should be consistent with the image that you are trying to convey and be consistent with the norms of your industry. For instance, go to the Google home page and you will see the bright colors of the Google name and logo. The multi-colored letters are distinctive and give a light and happy feel to your "search". These colors with the almost child-like imagery would not work well for a law firm which will need a very serious and sedate image, since all lawyers are boring by nature (just kidding, sort of).

Major design firm fees can add up to thousands of dollars for a logo design and are well worth it for consumer packaged-goods firms. For a small business, you can seek out a part-time designer or a starving art student. Alternatively, go to Google, enter the key words "logo design", and you will find hundreds of firms that design logos using templates. It will cost you less than a couple hundred dollars.

My designer friends are cringing right now.

This weekend: Grab a stack of magazines and look for product logos that appeal to you; cut them out and save them for future reference. What do they have in common?

42. Colors for Printed Materials, Logos, and Websites

"Creativity takes courage."

Henry Matisse (1869–1954) Artist

When designing printed materials, logos, and websites, many factors come into play. One factor of great importance is color since your brand is expressed through your choice of color. Color evokes a mood or feeling and must be chosen carefully. It must be consistent with the image that you want to communicate to your target audience.

Red is a call to action, is aggressive and can be exciting. It is a great color for logos and for accents when it is used with other more neutral background colors. It can clash with green, blue, and purple. It is best used with other warm colors like yellow, brown, or orange. Red demands attention; it says stop and come look at me. It is too strong for a background color since it would be irritating or overwhelming.

Black can be a depressing, if not a mournful color. It feels heavy. Yet, it can also be sophisticated and alluring; it can feel luxurious and prestigious. It functions well as a backdrop for an artist's work or with photographic images. It seems to go well with technical images or presentations. Black can be a great color for text on the website.

White is an excellent background for a professional business on a website. It denotes cleanliness, purity, and youth. It feels simple and innocent. Many of the best consumer websites choose white as the background of choice, Note that Google's home page is white and very simple; they spell out the Google name in primary colors making it fun, if not child-like.

Green is the color of nature and the environment. Light green is a great background for professional service firms like a law firm or a CPA firm. Green communicates safety and encourages you to go forward. Bright green is trendy right now for high tech firms; it has a retro feel that reminds us of the sixties.

Blue can create an image of tranquillity and peacefulness. Light blue is a common background for service-based businesses such as consulting firms; it communicates a calm solution. Blue can be authoritative while dark blue is heavy and morose; think police officer. Medium blue can also be over-the-top and goofy.

Beige is a great neutral color, which speaks of conservatism. By itself it is boring or plain. Paired up with accent colors like green or brown or blue, beige is very readable. Beige can make a super background, if complemented with the right accent colors.

Brown is a great color for text in print and on a website. Generally, brown is viewed as earthy or natural, while to others it might be dirty or dingy. Brown works well with green. It can also communicate a natural or rural or primitive look. Brown is warm and comfortable.

Yellow is the most irritating color out there and is great for getting your attention, but use it sparingly. Many great logos use yellow (often paired with red). Yellow is the color of cowardice or caution.

When choosing a color, you should consider the 216 colors supported by web browsers. It is generally recommended that you start with color choices compatible with the web palette and then consider color on paper. Go to Google and enter the words "web palette" and you will find all 216 vibrant colors. If you start with color on paper, it might not be found in the web palette. Consistency is a huge factor in building brand awareness with logos.

To do: Go surf the net looking for websites that look cool; save them by using your "favorites" tab for later use. What elements do they have in common that you like?

43. Good Brochures Need to be Written in Plain Language

"Many men go fishing all of their lives without knowing that it is not fish they are after."

Henry David Thoreau (1817–1862) Philosopher and author

Most brochures (and most business communications too) are boring, dripping with meaningless business jargon, and almost meaningless. Words and phrases such as "leading edge value proposition" or "extensible brand legacy" raise the question, "What does this stuff really mean?" Not much to me or most people. Combat this insult on the English language with simple, plain communication. This plain talk is especially important in brochures when your objective is to sell something or, at least, communicate.

Creating good brochures is hard work. Start by doing some research. What types of brochures is your competition using? What brochures look good to you? What shapes and sizes are used? What colors are standard in your industry, if any? A little bit of time devoted to this type of research will clarify your thoughts on what is important in a brochure's content and what looks good to you in terms of design. Ask others what they like about brochures.

A larger question to ask is what is the purpose of the brochure? Some brochures are designed for a prospect or new customer; this brochure wants to catch the attention of the reader quickly with a headline or graphic or photo. The call to action is for the prospect to contact you and discuss the solution. Other brochures perpetuate the dialog with a prospect or a customer; in the sales trade these brochures are called "leave behinds". While it is possible to accomplish both objectives in the same brochure, you might want to create two different brochures, if time and budget allow.

A good brochure speaks to the reader's wants and needs. Ask yourself, what is the reader looking for in my brochure? Often, the reader wants to know that you understand his or her need. I recommend starting a brochure with a statement about the problem, which needs solving. You could describe these words or phrases as a pain or symptom. This problem statement should be the front page of your brochure. The use of a question to pique the interest of the reader can be effective. The objective of the cover or first page is to get them to open the brochure. I have read that up to 70% of brochure readers won't open the brochure or go to page two. Thus, the front page must intrigue the readers, which means it must speak to them personally about their problem. This also means your company name and logo go at the bottom of the first page. (Some designers say page two.) Remember it is about them not you.

Page two is normally devoted to the product description. Try to avoid technical jargon as much as you can, since most buyers don't care or don't understand it anyway. Use benefits statements instead of technical specifications. If they need technical questions answered, a brochure won't be able to do the job in most cases. Direct them to your website or to a number to call. Technical specifications can quickly become out-of-date and should not be in the brochure anyway.

Most business communications are boring and amazingly similar. Make your brochure different so that it will be noticed. Generally speaking, four-color brochures are better for capturing and keeping attention. Try different shapes and sizes; this is very appropriate if the brochure's purpose is attract a new customer. Be careful of size and paper weight if you plan to self-mail this same brochure. Check with the post office so you don't inadvertently increase your postage cost by sending an oversized piece. Most brochures are 8 1/2 by 11; so, don't do that. One good thing about 8 1/2 by 11 brochures is that they fit nicely in a file folder. The purpose of your brochure is to show your reader that you are different, so break the rules.

I recommend writing the brochure as if you are writing to a friend. People buy from people. Eliminate all the clichés and trite business sayings. Write succinctly and briefly. Be sure to avoid putting too much information into the brochure, since whatever detail you choose to put in the brochure will likely not be what the customer wants. Leave lots of white space to help the reader find what is important; white space around a key point helps the reader find the statement or image and concentrate on it. Use short sentences, simple visuals and short paragraphs. Limit your paragraphs to no more than five or six lines with two or three sentences. Readers' eyes fatigue easily, so keep them going to the next paragraph or next page of the brochure. Unlike a book, don't indent paragraphs.

A few other things to consider:

- Typeface is hot issue in design circles, but I prefer to keep it simple. Use two typefaces at most.
- A common error in brochures is to make them too busy by emphasizing everything in the brochure. Simple is better. Avoid using too many bolded or underlined items for emphasis; when overdone, nothing is emphasized.

- Consider adding a FAQ (frequently asked questions) to your brochure. FAQ's are a great way to logically answer a prospect's questions about your solution. Readers will have questions and concerns about next steps and your solution in general. FAQ's are a great way to answer the fears and keep the customer reading.
- Carefully edit and proofread your copy. Misspellings and grammatical errors are unprofessional and unacceptable; also, you need to avoid incorrect verb tenses, dropped verbs, omitted words or punctuation, and non-standard capitalization. If you can afford it, have a professional proofreader review your document.
- Photography is a very specialized field. Make sure that your photographer has successfully done work in your industry. It can really make a difference.
- Many readers will only read the headlines in your brochure, so don't be subtle. Describe the benefits of your solution and what to do next. Always write as if the customer will buy your solution. Be direct and assumptive.
- Testimonials can help address fears that buyers may have about your firm or solution. Disburse testimonials throughout the brochure from start to finish. In fact, a testimonial is a great way to start a brochure and get them to go to page two. Place the testimonial near the feature or benefit that it supports.
- The back page of the brochure should have all contact information including website address, map with directions, street address, hours of operation, phone numbers, fax number, e-mail addresses and other pertinent stuff.

Do this every day: Keep a log of the questions your customers ask you about your firm. Write down the answers that you give back. This log will be the start of your new FAQ (frequently asked questions).

44. What is the Difference Between Selling and Marketing?

"Life is a matter of salesmanship."

Thomas J. Watson (1875–1956) Founder of IBM

I am frequently asked about the difference between selling and marketing.

Academically speaking, selling is a function of marketing, as is advertising, promotion, and pricing. (Reread the chapter on the 4 Cs and 4 Ps.) Practically speaking, marketing is what happens before the phone rings and selling is what happens after you answer the phone. Marketing is all about understanding the customer's needs, figuring out how to get the message out, and negotiating the competitive landscape. Selling is all about the needs of the firm and is product focused; the desired outcome is financial in nature.

Part of the confusion about the definitions of the terms is how corporate America tends to treat marketing and sales organizationally. Many firms tend to align marketing with the manufacturing operation, while disassociating the marketing function from the sales organization. The marketing organization tends to be lower paid, more technical, and is considered a staff function; the sales organization tends to be higher paid, more gregarious, and remotely located from the manufacturing plant. A chasm is created between the sales and marketing teams by this organizational design. Instead of working as a team to serve the client, marketing and sales do combat about what is right for the customer and which team should control the decision-making authority. Thus, the debate about what is sales and what is marketing is rooted in the politics of corporate America.

Luckily, small and medium sized businesses can organize sales and marketing as one department to avoid this type of conflict.

A little bit of philosophy: think marketing first, then sales. Marketing asks you to first think about the needs of the customer; sales asks you to focus on your product (if you are not careful).

45. Sales is a Process

"Nothing is more difficult than the art of maneuvering
for advantageous positions."

Sun-Tzu (544–496 B.C.) Chinese military strategist

No matter how you sell or what you sell, there is an underlying sales process that the buyer and the seller follow. Much like a ritual or dance, you must follow the basic steps to get the desired outcome, which is to close the sale. Although industries vary in the sales methods or channels used, the process is more or less the same.

The sales process begins with a first contact with the prospect; often this is accomplished with a marketing campaign. It is legend in sales that "frequency of contact" may be the most important factor in helping the buyer become comfortable with the idea of choosing your product. Advertising and public relations help accelerate this process of awareness by sending an ongoing message to the prospective customers. The message typically has a call to action, which describes an incentive for the prospect to contact the seller now. Incentives could include discounted pricing, compelling features or benefits, or a solution to a problem. The delivery method for this message could be e-mail, direct mail, phone, print, television, radio, or blog. Each target market has a unique mix of delivery methods that work best. Thus, the purpose of the marketing campaign is to create awareness for the provider's solutions and to create a call to action.

The next step in the selling process is called a lead. This is when the interested prospect takes action by contacting the seller or by agreeing to be contacted. A lead can be created by the buyer hitting the website, calling the toll free number, or by accepting the call from the telemarketer. Regardless of method, the selling has begun.

Maybe the most important step in the sales process is qualification. In this step, the sales representative follows up with the prospective buyer to determine if the prospect has the ability and need to make the purchase decision. More than likely, the sales representative will use open-ended questions to better understand the buyer's needs and motivations. For many industries, this qualification is done over the phone prior to meeting in person; yet, each industry is different. For example, in the automobile industry, prospective buyers are presumed qualified if they walk onto the dealership car lot. Basically, if a prospect shows up, automobile salespeople will assume that the buyer is ready and able to buy.

In simplest terms, a qualified buyer has the following characteristics:

- Responded to the call for action.
- Has a need that matches your product or solution.
- Has the authority (or access to the authority) to make the purchase decision.
- Has the budget to make the purchase.
- Can make the decision in a reasonable time frame.

Once qualification is complete, the process then focuses on a deeper discussion about the prospect's needs and how the seller's product can help. This discussion could include a demonstration of the product; in the automobile industry example, the prospective buyer could take a test drive around the block. For other industries, a detailed discussion of the customer's needs is required, along with a review of the seller's product specifications. In technology industries, this step may require both the buyer and the seller to bring in technical support to better determine the fit of the product.

Often at this stage, the buyer will ask difficult or probing questions about the seller's product; it is common for the buyer to express concern about the product's fit or the seller's ability to provide the best solution. These questions and concerns are called "objections"; in sales vernacular, objections are requests for information, since often the buyer needs to better understand the product before a purchase can be made. When a buyer speaks of a concern, the seller should respond by asking the buyer to tell more about the concern. For the seller, it very important to actively listen to the buyer's words. Repeating the buyer's words back to the buyer can demonstrate that you are listening and that you understand. This basic communication is critical to the buyer and seller.

Answering the objection should be done concisely and quickly. Although facts are important, answering the objection with a short story or an example may prove more powerful and more memorable. A story about how another buyer had the same concerns or questions, but who successfully made the purchase while solving their problems, could ease the buyer's concerns. To verify that you have answered the objection, the seller then needs to ask the buyer if there are any other concerns or questions. If the buyer has more questions, the process repeats itself. Each time the seller needs to verify that the objection has been resolved; the process cannot go forward until all questions are answered.

At this point in the sales process, some industries offer references from current customers; properly positioned references can be very powerful. Care must be taken when choosing the reference; candidly, your references must say the right things about your product so it makes sense to verify what they might say before hand. Other industries might offer a "proof of concept" or a trial at this stage; this is done to confirm the fit and to help the buyer to better understand the product. Presuming no more objections, the buyer is ready to go forward.

With all objections answered, the seller can move the sales process along by attempting a "trial close". A trial close verifies that all objections are answered and that the buyer is ready to buy. Often the seller will ask an open-ended question like "How do you feel about this?" Or, "How would you like to proceed?" Sometimes, these questions will draw out more objections. In that case, the questions must be answered and the seller must verify that the questions were fully answered. If the concerns are addressed, the seller can move on to the final close.

If the buyer is qualified and if the seller has answered all the objections from the buyer, then closing the sale is easy. Often the motivated buyer will want to call the shots and will take over the process. From my perspective, this means that the deal is nearly done. Some experienced buyers will patiently wait for the seller to ask the closing questions; they know the selling ritual and respect it. I don't mean to trivialize pricing and negotiation, but from a process perspective this is the normal flow for a sales process. I address pricing and negotiation in other chapters, so check them out.

The last step in the sales process is the delivery of the product or the beginning of the service contract. The order may have been "inked", but the selling must continue. For the entrepreneur, this is a critical step since good references are so important to future business in a niche market. At this stage, many organizations send the sales representative off to chase the next customer. I disagree whole-heartedly. The representative needs to be involved during the initial stages of the product installation; those first few weeks or months will determine if you buyer will buy again. The provider's goal should be to exceed customer expectations and earn the right to do business again with the customer.

Sales Tip: Speak to your customer in plain language and avoid business clichés. Treat them like a friend and you will be treated the same.

46. Listening to Customers

"I like to listen. I have learned a great deal from listening carefully.
Most people never listen."

Ernest Hemingway (1899–1961) Author and adventurer

When asked to describe the essential traits of a good salesperson, many people will first respond with "a gift for gab" (the ability to talk at length on cue). Nothing could be farther from the truth.

To sell most effectively, salespeople need to actively listen to what is important to the customer; nothing else really matters. Of course, saying the right things at the right time is very important in personal selling, but knowing what to say and when to say it is a function of listening first.

Active listening has three simple components. First, you need to hear what is said, which requires you to keep your mouth shut. The core objective is to be able to repeat what was said. The second objective is to understand. You can demonstrate understanding by generalizing about what was said. Finally, the third component of listening is to apply it to a real life situation.

Some hints on being a better listener with your customers:

- Stay in the moment. Make eye contact. Focus on what is being said.
- Don't let your mind wander. Avoid anticipating what will be said next or what you should say or ask next.
- It is good to nod, smile, and laugh to show the customer that you are listening. Be there, but don't talk, at least not yet.
- Don't interrupt or interject with smart thoughts or ideas. Customers like the chance to deliver their full message.
- Don't jump to false judgments or conclusions; let your speaker finish.
- Do your best to be neutral even if your speaker is rude or flying off the handle; focus on the message, not the delivery.
- Most customers communicate a few basic ideas when they speak; in fact, they will typically repeat them for you with cues such as "The most important thing is…" or "My point is…."
- If you are not sure what was said or just don't remember, ask clarification questions. This shows interest on your part and most people don't mind helping you understand their main points.

- When the customer is done, restate the main points and seek affirmation that you heard correctly. Ask questions that request a deeper understanding.

Seek to discover not to judge.

A simple exercise: Next time that you are with a customer, don't take any notes. Just listen. At the end of the conversation, repeat back your understanding to the customer. See if you listened.

47. Tell Stories to Your Customers

"If you've heard this story before, don't stop me, because I'd like
to hear it again."

Groucho Marx (1890–1977) Comedian and actor

Facts tell, while stories sell.

Have your salespeople tell stories. I have found that most successful
salespeople sell by telling stories and not by making presentations. And, it
does not seem like they are selling.

Top salespeople can build trust and credibility while overcoming
skepticism by talking about how another customer solved a problem by
using a product or service. A good story can address an objection or concern before the customer ever brings it up. Done right, the story well-told
makes the storyteller appear sincere and trustworthy.

Sales presentations are the quickest way to lose a sale since there may
be nothing more obvious or obnoxious than a canned pitch, better known
as "death by PowerPoint". Shut down the laptop and build the relationship
with your customer by sharing your stories.

Connect with a customer's emotions by talking about past experiences with other customers. Stories can be a great way to break the ice with
a new customer and ease the natural tension in a sales call. For the existing
client, the well-told tale can enrich the business relationship. Generally,
customers can identify with the story and can picture themselves as a part
of the story. This emotional connection helps them remember the story
while they may never remember the facts or figures, let alone the features
and benefits of your product. Stories should have a simple theme or value;
if the tale is too complicated the message could get lost.

The mechanics are simple. A good story's opening is clear and engag-
ing. The sequence of events must be easy to follow. Don't be too clever or
you might lose your audience. The story must have a clear ending and must
have had a purpose. If done right, the story lives on in the memory of your
customer. Story telling can achieve things that marketing brochures can't.

Be sure to tell true stories and not tall tales. An outlandish fib or an
outright lie will be immediately visible and self-defeating. Keep a record of
all your stories. This preserves the stories for use by others in your firm and
it will protect the facts within the story. A good use of the archived stories
could be to help your new employees learn about your firm's value propo-

sition. Or, when properly edited, these stories could go on your website for viewing by visitors.

One more thought: Stories don't all need happy endings. Sad stories can help us learn and teach others.

48. Why Customers Buy?

"Customers buy for their reasons, not yours."

Unknown

Different customers buy for different reasons. From a psychological perspective, people buy because of four underlying reasons that may not be visible on the surface:

- "Needs" are things that you must have to survive and to function; this includes shelter, food, clothing, and medicine. These purchases are easily justified and are basic motivations for a buyer.
- "Wants" are things that are desired, but not necessary such as wanting an iPod. Wants are tougher for the buyer to justify, but people will buy them because of an innate ability to rationalize most any purchase. If I buy an iPod I will be happier and more popular.
- "Desires" are wishes or dreams, which can be powerful motivators. You can desire to be famous and this can motivate you take to action or not to take action. Desires can motivate people to change or modify their behavior. If you lose weight, you will be more attractive and this can help make you famous.
- "Fear" can motivate the buyer to take action or not to take action. Fear can create barriers to success by holding people back from taking a promotion. Or, fear can also keep people safe by keeping them from taking unnecessary risks; if you don't buy this book, you will not be successful, so you buy it out of fear.

At the salesperson's level, these underlying needs of the buyer are not always visible. What the salesperson senses or observes is the more top-level buying motivations such as:

- "Technical superiority" or innovation is a desire-based motivation for those who want to be important.
- "To please the boss" is a fear-based motivation.
- "Peer pressure" can manifest itself as "everyone else is buying it, so I should too"; this may be based on a desire to be loved.
- "Status or prestige" buyers say, "I want the best"; this is a desire to be important.

- "Policy" is a common fear motivation. They will justify the wrong decision since this is the way they always do things. ("Welcome to the U.S. Postal Service.")
- To "justify an opinion or decision" already made; this seems more needs based to me.
- "Excess budget" is needs based since they need to spend the money to preserve the budget for next year.
- Fear of making a wrong decision. Yep, this is plain old fear.

Why is your prospect going to buy from you? Probe more deeply to understand why they will buy your service or product. You need to remember that buyers don't buy products because of you, but because of their needs, wants, fears, or desires. Remember it is all about them.

Your to do list: Next time you are with a customer, who recently bought your product or service, ask them why they bought from you, instead of the competition.

49. Whom Do We Trust?

"Without trust there is nothing."

Unknown

We all know trust when we see it or feel it or smell it (literally), for trust is very mammalian. We seem to be born with a special sense for estimating the trustworthiness of other people or groups of people.

For whatever reason, we seem to trust some people right away (likely just a few), while all others have to earn our trust. You know what I mean. Right away, we trust some individuals and it may be hard to explain other than it feels OK to do so. And, sometimes we are right and sometimes we are wrong.

Would you buy something from someone you don't trust? Most people won't. Studies have shown that lack of trust may disable a sale more quickly than any other factor. So, what is trust? In my words, it is the feeling you get from someone when what they say equals what they do. You come to this conclusion by some initial sense or by monitoring their behavior. You can observe it by watching what people say and do; I guess it is kind of like keeping score. We do this whether we are aware of it or not.

For salespeople trying to crack a new account, building trust can be time-consuming and difficult. In most instances, trust is earned by making promises and by delivering on those promises. It may take awhile.

Think of some examples of people that seem trustworthy: Mother Teresa, former President Jimmy Carter, kindergarten teachers, firemen, and former network anchorman, Walter Cronkite. For many, we have learned to trust them because of our past experiences with them. We find their behavior consistent, reliable, and acceptable.

How about used car sales people, gang members, most politicians, and insurance agents? Most of us don't trust these people. We have learned not to trust them because of their behavior.

So, how do you demonstrate trustworthiness?

- Be specific in what you promise and only promise what you can truly deliver.
- Use lots of eye contact.
- Speak slowly and clearly.
- Listen and repeat back what the other person wants, "So, let me make sure that I understand; what is important to you is…."

- Do exactly what you said would you would do. No exceptions.
- Report back to the person that you had made the promise and tell them what you did. This confirms your commitment and this communication is a further demonstration of your trustworthiness.
- If you did not meet your commitment, tell them immediately; this disclosure is the behavior of a trusted person. Don't try to hide the mistake or delay in telling them; you are certain to get caught and then you will have lost any chance of building a trust-based relationship.
- Repeat until you are trusted; this may take awhile.

For a business, earning a prospect's trust follows the same formula. Cracking the trust barrier with the new customer is all about frequency of contact; every single contact is an opportunity to demonstrate your firm's trustworthiness by doing what you promised when you promised. But, you must be patient. Studies have shown that it can take on average 16 to 20 contacts before a customer feels comfortable in buying from a new provider. This is why large consumer products firms pour millions of dollars into advertising; they know that they have to invest in getting to know their new customers.

Keeping the trust of the current customer is all about maintenance; it is the responsibility of the provider to deliver the goods on time as promised. Nothing will unravel the established trust as much as promising to deliver something that could not be delivered; worse yet, is hiding the fact, lying about it or making up excuses. After you lose trust, getting it back is harder than starting from scratch.

My advice? Do the right thing.

One more thought: Ask yourself, "Whom do you trust? Why them?"

50. *Channel of Distribution: How to Sell Your Product or Services*

"There are worse things in life than death. Have you ever spent an evening with an insurance salesman?"

Woody Allen (1935–) Comedian, author, and director

"Channel of distribution" is a fancy term for the individual, group or firm that manages or conducts the necessary activities and actions to sell a product or service. The channel delivers the product or service to the customer. Simply put, channel of distribution is how a business sells products and services. And, there are many options for a business to consider.

The most common choice is direct sales; with this option, the firm owns the resource. The direct sales approach is usually the most expensive method, but it is the most knowledgeable channel. Direct sales employees can be inside sales reps on the phone or field sales reps making in-person sales calls. This method allows the most control over the day-to-day activities including the number of calls, what is said or presented to the customer, and how the customer is treated.

Another common method used is the representative model, which is typically a "commission only" relationship with an independent sale rep or sales organization that sells within a geographical territory. Commonly known as a "rep firm" or manufacturer's rep, they often sell multiple products, which typically do not compete with each other.

There are many advantage of having a rep firm sell your product or service. Rep firms tend to be staffed with sales veterans who have special knowledge of your target customer, of the product line itself, and are highly skilled salespeople. They can be inside sales or outside sales or a combination of both; they tend to have long-standing relationships with the customers and provide the business immediate access to buyers. Rep firms can be a great way for a small business to get started since you pay them only for what they sell (i.e., since they are commission only).

There are also disadvantages of using rep firms. A big negative is share of mind; with other lines in their portfolio, you compete with the other product lines for their time. A good rep firm will focus their energy on where the commission is most available. With many lines, they have many masters and many times they are spread very thin. They are smart and they know a lousy product when they see it; a smart rep will ignore a product that does not sell well or quickly.

Distributors are typically large professional sales organizations with inside and outside sales. They stock inventory and sell on behalf of the manufacturer. Often, they carry many different and often competing product lines. You can think of this type of channel as a financial institution, which has the objective of turning inventory as many times as possible. They can be national, regional, or local. Like the rep firm, the distributor can employ highly skilled salespeople who have special access to customers; they typically have inside and outside salespeople. Share of mind is also an issue with the distributor, since they may have dozens of lines to sell.

Dealers sell multiple product lines with an inside or outside sales staff and have a restricted geographical footprint. They seldom take inventory. Dealers tend to have exclusive agreements for product. They typically have special sales expertise such as technical ability or customer knowledge.

Similar to a dealer is a Value Added Reseller (VAR). VARs will sell your product bundled with other products as a total solution. In the software industry, a VAR might market accounting software with PC products to a target market. They bring a special knowledge of the application along with access to customers. Sometimes, they will add their own product solutions into the mix.

Brokers are independent sales reps or sales organizations, which are similar to manufacturer's reps. Mostly, the name is changed, but in some industries brokers have special licenses or certification. Brokers are common in the food, insurance, and loan industries. They are commission only and tend to be highly specialized in geography, vertical, or niche.

Channel partners are sales partners who call on the same customer that you do and can influence the customer to consider your services. Typically, channel partners are a source of leads and not actual sales. Channel partners are the current rage in technology circles. For example, having Intel as a channel partner can open up doors instantly for a new technology venture.

Franchisees are licensed sellers of a product or service. Often used in retail, this approach utilizes the financial resources of an independent business to sell to a target market. Using a proven formula, the franchisor controls the marketing of the product or service by requiring stringent rules on use of the licensed methods by the franchisees.

Retail stores are another channel of distribution. Typically these are company-owned stores staffed with the firm's employees. This compares closely with the direct sales channel, but is limited to a strictly retail marketing effort.

Frankly, I have only scratched the surface on the subject of channel distribution; the names vary greatly from industry to industry.

Homework assignment: Analyze the sales channels used by your competitors; are they the same as yours? Are they better?

51. Channel Strategies: Which Combination Works Best?

"The jungle is dark, but full of diamonds."

Arthur Miller (1915–) Playwright

So, with all these varieties of distribution channels, which is best for small business? You will find that different industries have preferred methods, so that choice may be already made for you.

Most businesses will choose a channel strategy that best fits their target market. A one-channel approach will allow the firm control of the quality of the sales process; this might be the direct or rep firm approach. Often in this case, the target market is finite and significant product knowledge is needed to sell product.

When do you go direct versus rep? The quick answer is when control is necessary. Some products or services need extraordinary attention and technical knowledge from the sales force to get the product sold. Another good use of a direct sales model is when the sale happens well in advance of the financial transaction. For example, the design-in cycle for electronic equipment can take place many months in advance of when the product ships and before commissions are paid. A direct sales force can be salaried to work with the customer's engineering team and get the product designed-in without worrying about their paycheck.

Otherwise, a rep firm can be an outstanding choice to get instant access to customers, to get a skilled senior sales staff, and to get your sales effort launched. Rep firms get paid only when they sell, so they can be a very cost-effective way to sell while managing your cash flow. Rep firm commission rates vary from industry to industry, but the overall payout is comparable to a direct sales organization. When sales volumes become large, there can be cost savings by switching to a direct sales model.

A multiple-channel strategy is often used when a firm is serving many customers in a large geographic area. A typical multi-channel strategy could include the use of direct sales at major or existing accounts with distributors covering the smaller accounts or distantly located accounts. Channel conflict can be a problem with this approach since there can be situations where both channels can claim the same order and demand commissions. This type of conflict is avoided by strict rules of engagement on what constitutes a commissioned event and who owns which customer.

Action: Ask your customer if they can recommend any good sales-people. Call them up and ask them to join you for lunch.

52. E-mail Marketing Techniques That Will Increase Revenue Today

"For believe me, the secret of harvesting from existence the greatest fruitfulness and greatest enjoyments is to live dangerously."

Friedrich Nietzsche (1844–1900) Philosopher

Many businesses rely on e-mail to sell their goods and services, since e-mail is cheap and quick; yet, the effectiveness of e-mail selling can be quite disappointing. To improve your effectiveness when marketing with e-mail, I recommend the following suggestions:

- First, the goal is get the customer to contact you, so give them a reason do so. Build campaigns that pique interest and that provide value. The call to action for the customer could be for more information, a discount if they act now, or a free item.
- Be creative with your subject header, but be specific on the purpose of the e-mail. Let them know why you are contacting them, since trying to fool them into reading your e-mail will backfire. Also, use no more than forty characters in your subject header.
- The quality of your e-mail list is directly correlated to your success. How old is this list? Have your contacts given their permission to be e-mailed back? Have they shown an interest in your products or services?
- The best choice is using your own list, which includes names you have collected. Document how you got the names and when you got them. Keep this information on file permanently.
- One technique that is really successful is to personalize the subject header with the recipient's name or a quote that he or she made to the press. Just about everyone can be tracked down on Google these days. Find a quote that they made to the press or dig up some personal anecdote about them. Put this in the subject header. If your prospect coaches little league, use a reference to little league. I bet that they will open it.
- Never include your company name in the subject line. When you include your company, your name, or your solution in the subject header, you send a loud message that you want to sell something now. Remember it is not about you; rather, it is all about the customer.

- Your e-mails should provide value to the reader. Value can delivered by being timely or by offering information that is helpful. Other things that could be viewed as valuable could include notification about a sale, a discount, or a free sample.
- Create intimacy by writing to your prospect as a person. Write like you are writing to a friend. Drop the formality of business language and use words like you, we, and us. Use a conversational tone with plain, simple words.
- Be careful about offending the reader by using overly casual language. In particular, the reader can easily misinterpret slang or sarcasm. And, you never know exactly who will be reading your e-mail. Remember this is business.
- Make sure the opening paragraph or opening sentence of the body of e-mail ties to the header. This consistency reassures the reader that the e-mail will deliver the promise of the subject header.
- Focus on the reader's pain or needs, not your solution. Demonstrate your knowledge of the reader's issues. This is not the time for sales pitches. Focus the message on the issues and problems that you believe your prospects are having.
- Most readers don't read e-mails, they skim or scan them. Use short paragraphs and with lots of white space to separate the paragraphs. This technique makes it easier for the reader to find what they are looking for.
- HTML looks better than plain text, makes for a better layout, and allows images to be inserted into the message. This can lead to a higher response rates. When using HTML or graphic images, beware of slowing down the loading of the message. Some people just won't wait, so don't overdo your e-mail design.
- Your e-mail should have a simple call to action which should be to call you, e-mail you, or go to your website. Give the e-mail a purpose.
- E-mail may not be the best way to sell to decision makers. It's best to think of e-mail as a way to create new relationships, rather than as selling. Set your expectations accordingly.
- Be concise. Stick with a one-page or a one-screen length limit for your e-mail message. If you make your message longer, your reader likely won't read it anyway. This is controversial within the e-mail marketing community, since if you connect with your reader, he or she will want to read more. Some experts suggest that a longer e-mail is the right thing to do. In my opinion, this is when they should click on a link and visit your website. E-mail is a means, not an end.

- Give your reader an "opt-out" or unsubscribe instructions for your e-mail at the bottom of your e-mail. The Can-Spam Act of 2003 (which went into effect in 2004) requires that all e-mail messages contain clear directions on how to opt-out from subsequent mailings. Provide an unsubscribe mechanism that allows those receiving your e-mail to opt-out from receiving further e-mails from you or your business.
- Beware of long distribution lists. One way to avoid this problem is to use a bcc; this way the names won't be shown.
- Be sure to include your contact information. This should include all the basics: name, address, website, phone, etc.
- Postscripts are a great way to finish with an additional announcement or comment, such as a special event coming up with you as a speaker. Postscripts get read.
- Always use spell check and be sure to proofread since spell check will miss errors, such as using "their" instead of "there". Spell check won't catch omitted words either.
- Some entrepreneurs will admit to having poor writing skills or "writer's block". One way around this issue to delegate the task to someone on your staff who has writing skills and the interest. You can function as the editor while delegating the writing chore. Have the staff member interview you and come back with an article; you can edit it for accuracy. Another tip is to call the local college to a find a starving student with writing skills; their wages will be modest and they need the job experience.

Your action: Review your e-mail campaigns from the last year. Which ones were most successful? What did the successful campaigns have in common?

53. Have You Checked Out eBay?

"They've finally come up with the perfect office computer. If it makes a
mistake, it blames another computer."

Milton Berle (1908–2002) Comedian

Many businesses choose eBay as primary or secondary channel of
distribution, which can provide instant access to a mass audience. I have
heard estimates that up to a million people make money selling on eBay. A
year ago, I might have said that only certain types of businesses can market their products or services on eBay. I think I have changed my mind.
Today, diamonds, insurance, and homes are sold on eBay.

Here are a few tips for using this exciting approach:

- Make sure to do all the business basics including the setup of a
  legal business. Many eBay entrepreneurs are shoppers who first
  got hooked and then started selling. Soon the hobby takes on a
  life of its own.
- Play customer on eBay and make a few purchases so that you
  understand the experience. The role of service is huge for an
  internet transaction.
- Consider using auctions as a way to promote your eBay store; if
  you routinely use eBay, a storefront is easy and inexpensive to set
  up. Consider the auction process as the hook or promotion that
  helps people to find your store. After they find your store, your
  merchandise, service, and quality will keep them coming back.
- Price smart, not stupid. Remember that is an auction environment
  and people are bargain hunting. This may not be a best channel
  for value-based products, but what I like about it is the immedi-
  acy of the feedback.
- Amazingly, the big retailers have discovered eBay; they use eBay
  to sell old or excess merchandise. Many businesses use eBay as
  a channel to dump old, imperfect, or unwanted inventory. This
  may work for you too. Some firms use a different brand name on
  eBay.
- Set up a PayPal account, since you will need to offer people a
  way to pay. It is easy to do and it's free.
- Spend the time and money for good photographs of your merchandise. This will help sell your product. Also, be sure to give

very specific product or service descriptions since this is an e-mail environment. People need to fully understand a product before they will buy it. Also, be sure to describe all flaws or imperfections on used or imperfect merchandise.

- Compelling titles or headlines are everything when it comes to listing your product on eBay; include key words in your eBay title. In fact, eBay's search software functions just like any other search engine. Avoid using trite or cliché words in the title such as low price, wow, or buy me. Instead, determine the words that most describe your offering and its benefits.
- Use eBay to promote your website; provide an opt-in newsletter to drive people to your site.
- Guarantees help overcome the fears of potential customers about buying your merchandise. This is a big deal in the eBay channel since many buyers remain suspicious about the vendors. Additionally, eBay has a ranking service that tracks buyers' feedback on eBay sellers; these rankings are critical to the success of the eBay sellers.
- Consider the use of testimonials; audio testimonials are proving to provide a big selling advantage on eBay.
- Have an "about us" or "about me" description or tab for your buyers on your site; people want to know who they are buying from. A "just us folks" style works well on eBay.
- Niche market products fit eBay. A niche marketer can sell used or hard-to-find items. There seems to be a market for everything on eBay: vacuum tubes, used cowboy lariats, and old software instruction manuals. If you can ship it, you can sell it on eBay.
- Check out the eBay resources for starting up a store; eBay offers a plethora of services on how to create a store, who to target, how to position your store, and how to avoid pitfalls in scaling an eBay store. Go to www.ebay.com/university for the real skinny on starting up a store on eBay.
- Go to http://pages.ebay.com/help/newtoebay/getting-started.html for more information on getting started on eBay.

When you have a minute: Go to eBay and search for products similar to yours. You may be surprised.

54. Farmers Farm and Hunters Hunt

"Don't confuse selling with art."

Jack Taylor, vice chairman of Jordan, McGrath, quoted in Randall Rothenberg, WHERE THE SUCKERS MOON: AN ADVERTISING STORY (1994)

Farming versus hunting is a topic of hot debate in the business press. The definitions of farmers and hunters are vague at best, but let me summarize my thoughts on the differences between the two styles.

Farmers are salespeople who value long-term relationships, exude patience, confidence, and determination, and can easily bounce back from rejection. The farmer sales rep sees the long-term benefit of doing business with a customer and can let "no" be an acceptable answer for now while waiting for "yes" later. This acceptance of the word "no" is key, since it takes the heat off the buyer and allows the business relationship to continue, if not enrich. The buyer learns to trust the farmer sales type and will even help the farmer rep out at quarter-end with higher prices or increased orders since they are friends. Given the nature of the relationship, the buyer also knows that when times are tough, the farmer rep will sacrifice orders today or accept order cancellations. The farmer and the buyer often jointly decide how to manage "order droughts" together. In effect, the farmer and buyer are partners.

On the other side of the tracks, lives the hunter sales rep. Aggressive by nature, the hunter is charming and can be very dominant. The hunter rep is egocentric and can be selfish; he or she is impatient and tends to interrupt other people when they speaking. The hunter has difficultly accepting "no" and is willing to sacrifice the relationship to get the order now. The hunter has a high action-orientation and is characterized by high sales activity. The buyer likes the hunter because the rep is charming, gets things done, and is efficient. When the work is done, the hunter leaves. This is a more traditional vendor/buyer relationship.

In practice, most sales reps have both farmer and hunter characteristics and seldom are reps purely one style or the other. So, which is best? I think it depends on your product or service and the type of buyer.

If your product or service is built on repeat business and service, the farmer profile may fit best. If the buyer needs the support of a long-term relationship from a flexible provider, the farmer rep will be a better choice. Examples of this would be pharmaceutical sales reps that routinely call on physicians, or printing sales reps that service print buyers.

If your sales organization is new business-focused or is a one-time sale, the hunter profile could be a better fit. Examples of this could be capital equipment sales or financial product sales. In this case, the buyer needs to do business now and needs the aggressive yet efficient execution of the hunter rep.

Determining the sales profile of a prospective rep that you are interviewing may not be simple. In truth, most sales reps have both hunter and farmer characteristics, but generally they will lean more to one of the two profiles. I recommend a review of the rep's job history to determine types of sales jobs the rep had and the success level attained. Where has the prospective rep worked before and whom did he or she sell to? Was he or she new business focused or existing accounts focused?

You may discover that a rep with an inconsistent job history may have been miscast in the wrong sales job. For example, an aggressive hunter may go to work in an industry that is characterized by long-term relationships and continuous service; the hunter's hard-charging style is a long-term misfit and the rep quickly burns through the territory. The same misfit can apply to the farmer in reverse who is hired as a hunter; lacking a sense of urgency, the farmer spends too much time taking care of relationships and not enough time making cold calls.

To avoid this misfit in your organization, take a hard look at the activities needed for success in sales at your firm. Do you need new accounts or do you need to penetrate existing accounts? Audit your current sales organization and study the high performers to determine their behavioral characteristics such as patience, aggressiveness, dominance, and flexibility. Create the profile of an optimum performer and do your best to hire reps that fit that profile.

Homework assignment: Do a stack ranking of your salespeople. Who is the best and why? Why are you are keeping the low performers?

55. The 7 Traits of Highly Successful Salespeople

"If winning isn't everything, why do they keep score?"

Vince Lombardi (1913–1970) Football coach

The difference between winning and losing in sales is often just a small margin. What makes that difference? I think it boils down to the following seven traits shared by successful salespeople:

1. Pedigree—Your sales reps must be winners and must have a history of winning. If you want a winner, hire one. Life is short and I don't recommend giving a failed sales rep a second chance. Look for a proven track record of success and be ready to pay top dollar. It is worth it.

2. High Activity—Given a choice between high activity and great selling skills, I will take high activity every day. Activity is within the control of the rep and can make up for mediocre skills. Maybe the best example of an activity is prospecting, while a good example of a selling skill is closing. A mediocre closer can still be a top rep if sufficient activity is there. The converse is not true.

3. Story Telling Ability—Customers respond to stories of how other customers have solved similar problems. I think that this skill can be taught but it takes a certain charisma to pull off a good story. Charisma is hard to teach.

4. Character—Successful sales reps communicate to the customer with a sense of great honesty and integrity. This makes the sales rep more believable and ultimately trusted. Making promises and delivering on those commitments earn this trust.

5. Strong Ego—The best reps that I have encountered want to be the best and are committed to doing what it takes to achieve that goal. This ambition can make them challenging to manage at times, but this desire to achieve is what fuels them.

6. Bravery—Great reps have boldness or fearlessness that propels them out of their comfort zone risking repeated rejection. When they encounter a barrier, they either overcome it or just walk around it.

7. Optimism—Successful reps see the future as bright. Setbacks are viewed as minor interruptions in their quest for excellence. They can have a tendency to "over forecast", but you can tolerate that.

One more thing: Most good salespeople are continuous learners; help them improve with off-site sales training. Everybody needs a tune-up, including the high achievers.

56. The Rebound Effect: Effective Handling of Customer Complaints

"Your most unhappy customers are your greatest source of learning."

Bill Gates (1955–) Founder of Microsoft

How you handle a customer complaint is often far more important than what the customer has complained about. It is legend that most customers don't bother to complain, instead they just go away. I have heard about studies that found that over 90% of unhappy customers don't care enough to complain.

Customers choose not to complain for many reasons. They think that it is not worth the trouble. They think no one cares. They are not sure how to complain. They think complaining will do no good and that you don't care. They may know you or like you and are afraid to complain. So, they don't complain. Instead, they choose to take their business elsewhere. So, when a customer complains, be honored that they are giving you another chance to satisfy their needs. Surveys show that over 50% of complaining customers end up staying with their current provider, if the provider handles the complaint well.

Meanwhile, the unhappy customer is predisposed to tell the world about their unhappiness. Studies show that the unhappy customer will tell up to ten other people about their unhappy experience. Given the instantaneous communication of the internet, those ten people will hear about it immediately. This bad word of mouth can be a tragedy to a business since referrals are such an important part of buying. By the way, the same study found that the happy customer would tell five people of their good experiences with a product or solution. In fact, if you can handle the complaint with dignity and sincerity, you will likely keep the customer. There is something cathartic about an honest discussion on the merits of your product or service that will enrich the relationship between customer and provider.

When a customer complains, you must drop everything and get with them in person, if possible. Now is the time to listen; now is not the time to speak. Let the rant begin. The customer needs to unload and you need to carefully absorb what is being said. Although notes can be taken, the customer will likely tell you a dozen times what went wrong and what you need to do to make it right. Make good eye contact and be prepared to eat humble pie.

If the complaint is over the phone or via a letter, treat it with same sense of urgency. Maintain a calm and respectful tone of voice; a friendly voice may sooth the unhappy customer. Whatever you do, do not argue. Of course, in most situations like this, there will be two sides of the story. Possibly the client abused the product or didn't follow instructions properly. The best thing is to listen and repeat the basics back to the client to demonstrate your understanding.

Presuming that the problem is correctable, the next step is to commit to an action plan that makes things better. Options could be to the test the product (i.e. do a post mortem) or research your work process to figure out what went wrong. Regardless of the next step, be sure to agree to a time line and then get it done on time or before.

Report back to the customer with your findings, your recommendations, and suggestions. Expect more ranting. When you cannot quickly resolve the customer complaint, be sure to call back with progress reports. Keep careful notes of your updates, commitments, and actions. My experience is that seldom does a client invest in a rant and not want to make things better. The outcome will likely be a stronger relationship based on this honest feedback and your professional response.

This is why doing customer satisfaction research is so important. When I speak with entrepreneurs about doing customer satisfaction research, the typical response is that they already talk to customers all the time and already know how they feel. If that is true, why do we get surprised when a customer leaves or chooses another vendor? Answer: the entrepreneur did not truly know what the customer was thinking.

Customer complaints can be opportunities to create better relationships. In addition, this exchange can make your product or solution better. An unhappy customer can help you fix a problem that could make the rest of your customers unhappy, only this time you get the chance to hear about it. Make it easy for customers to complain. Instead of avoiding the unhappy customer, give the unhappy customer a number to call. Complaint procedures could be included in product packaging, in contracts, on sales slips, in product manuals, on invoices, and even in your advertising.

Create awareness within your firm on how to handle unhappy customers with the creation of a complaint policy and procedure; call it "how to handle customer complaints". Think of the damage that a poorly trained employee could do by mishandling complaints.

Make the complaint feedback actionable by using it to make your product or solution better. Track complaints by product, salesperson, type of customer, etc. Are there any trends in these complaints? Could there be a product quality problem? Was the advertising misleading? What could be done next time to avoid this complaint?

After resolving the customer complaint, follow up with a phone call. Always send a personal note thanking them for stepping forward and let them know to call you anytime, anywhere.

Homework assignment: Call back all your customers that complained in the last six months; tell them that you are "just checking in".

57. "No" Can Be an Acceptable Answer

"Patience is the companion of wisdom."

St. Augustine (354–430) Philosopher

"No" is an acceptable answer in sales; usually it is simply a request for more information.

When beginning a new relationship with a prospective customer, the buyer often needs to say "no", at least for now. Let the buyer know that "no" is an acceptable answer since you are there to begin a long-term relationship, and you can wait for the order. Try this and you will see the buyer physically relax and smile. The pressure is off. This allows the conversation now to loosen up and the selling to begin. By taking the pressure off the buyer, the buyer can more freely discuss what is important. Of course, this helps you craft a better sales pitch.

Sometimes "no" means that you need to change your sales pitch. By probing more deeply into the "why" behind the "no", you may discover your prospective customer did not truly understand you, or you did a poor job of communicating. By accepting "no", you can improve your presentation and maybe get a second chance.

Other times, "no" means your product or solution is not a good fit for a particular customer. By digging deeper to understand why, you can learn which customers will fit your product best and which will not. This can make you more efficient in your selling. There may also be an opportunity to improve or change your product or solution.

Your assignment: Next time the customer says "no", ask them why?

58. When is a Customer Too Big?

"I once shot an elephant in my pajamas; how he got in my pajamas
I'll never know."

Groucho Marx (1890–1977) Comedian and author

Talk about a high-class problem. You have delivered a specialized solution in a niche market while doing all the right things this book recommends. What happens? You land an elephant for a customer who has an insatiable appetite for your product or service. By comparison, your other customers look like mice. You hate to admit it, but this customer has incredible influence over your day-to-day decisions, as well as your long term plans for the firm. Secretly, you live in fear that you might lose this giant customer overnight and find yourself out of business.

This is hard one for a small firm. I have seen many small firms prisoner to the revenue stream from one key customer. The reliance on a huge customer can impact the small firm's cash flow and control its day-to-day decisions, if not its destiny. If the big customer does not pay its bills on time, the firm can struggle to make payroll. When the big customer becomes too dominant, it can direct the day-to-day scheduling of activity, which might sacrifice the needs of other customers. At some point, the small business seemingly has no control over its destiny since the big customer is calling all the shots.

A general rule of thumb is that no one customer should account for more than 25 % of your sales. If a large customer abruptly drops you, you can still right-size your operation until you can find other sources of revenue. Even 25% makes me shudder, but in most cases, you can still adjust to the loss of this dominant customer. It will hurt, but the firm could still survive, presuming that you moved quickly enough.

Better yet, I recommend that you avoid this situation by selecting a target market small enough for you to be successful and big enough for you to choose your customers. I further recommend directing your marketing efforts to avoid this reliance on one large customer. Invest in diversity by delivering your message and focusing your sales effort on other prospective customers. Obviously, you want to avoid dancing too closely with the elephant, since it might step on you.

Your challenge: If you have a client that represents more than 25% of your revenue or one that will represent 25% of your sales soon, carefully invest in new business development elsewhere. Be sure to support your large client as usual.

59. Can I Count on You
for a Good Reference?

"Men of genius are admired, men of wealth are envied, men of power are feared; but only men of character are trusted."

Author unknown

If you ranked all the tools in the marketing tool bag, which include promotion techniques, pricing, advertising, channels of distribution, and public relations, you will find that reference accounts top the list in effectiveness. The most believed and trusted form of marketing, reference accounts are the best way to convince a prospect to try your solution. Let your happy clients do your selling for you.

When your firm is brand new, I encourage you to give away your product or service if that is what it takes to get a strong reference account. Consider doing business "pro bono" as my lawyer friends call it. Give it away and service the heck out of them in exchange for a good reference.

Peer references resonate because prospects find them believable. Meanwhile, the prospect is disinclined to believe the sales rep, even though the rep may truly be expert on the subject and may know far more than the buyer. This also explains why advertising is such an inefficient tool: it is obviously paid for by the sponsoring firm and is not believable. Likewise, the buyer knows that the rep is paid to sell. References provide a workaround for this trust problem.

By the way, the venture capital community figured out about reference accounts a long time ago. They frequently build portfolios of firms that sell to each other and act as reference accounts for each other. A little incestuous you proclaim? I agree. Nevertheless, it works and I guess all is fair when it comes to the VCs.

No better salesperson exists than the happy customer. Reference accounts are critical to the successful marketing effort at any business.

A fun thing to do: Next time a customer tells you what a great job that you have done, ask for a reference.

60. Selling to C-Level Executives Takes Preparation

"I never forget a face, but in your case I'll be glad to make an exception."

Groucho Marx (1890–1977) Comedian and author

The new millennium executive, particularly the C-level executive (i.e., CEO, CMO, CIO, etc.), needs a different sales approach. Gone are the days when the sales rep could have "discovery calls" with the C-level executive to better understand "pains" and key initiatives. Today, this senior-level buyer has no time for idle banter or conversation. The phone is ringing, the Blackberry is vibrating, and the in-box is bulging with unanswered e-mails.

Therefore, you have to adjust your sales approach. Sometimes you only get one shot with this character, so you have to be prepared. This necessitates that you thoroughly research the customer prior to discussing business. This means scouring the website, the SEC documents (if the firm is public), and calling others in the firm to learn about the real issues at play.

Anyone at the firm can be a source of useful information. The best people to talk with may be the C-level executive's direct reports. Call them and confide in them that you are meeting the "big guy" in two weeks and that you are trying to figure things out. What are his hot points? What do they recommend that you do to prepare? Who else should you talk to before the meeting? Some of these people actually will actually coach you on how to proceed. It can be that easy.

When you actually get together with the C-level executive, the meeting becomes a forum for you to demonstrate your knowledge of the firm and of the executive's key issues. This will pave the way for a constructive conversation and help move the sale along. This approach is time-consuming, but worth it when selling products or services that require you to call on top executives.

C-level executives are tough to get in front of, but once they get convinced to do business with you, they like to take over the sales process. This is called "transferring ownership" and it is a wonderful thing. It is a magic moment in selling when your customer joins you in the sales process while taking responsibility for the sales itself. For whatever reason, the customer now owns the sale along with you; the value has been demonstrated to such an extent that the customer takes over and makes it happen. Objections are resolved and the questions have been answered. When the C-level executive has accepted the ownership of the sales process, let him take control; victory is at hand.

Action item: Next time you get an appointment to call on a C-level executive, slow yourself down. Call up others in the organization and do some homework. Dazzle the executive with your knowledge of his issues when you present.

61. Tips for Getting Appointments by Phone

"Well, if I called the wrong number, why did you answer the phone?"

James Thurber (1894–1961) Author

It starts with a first phone call. For most of us in sales, the objective is finding the decision maker and getting an appointment. This is a lot harder than it sounds. Often the first person that we contact is called the gatekeeper; this individual is minding the store and their job is to keep us away from the decision maker. The gatekeeper has many titles depending on the size of the company that you are calling on. Titles could include secretary, administrative assistant, office manager, etc. What they all have in common is the goal to keep you away from the decision maker. A natural reaction is to consider this person to be an enemy.

Rather than treating the gatekeeper as an enemy, I suggest that you employ them as part of your selling team. This friendly approach will be welcomed since generally the gatekeepers are not used to being treated with respect. Enlist the gatekeeper to help you find valuable information. Treat them kindly by sending thank you cards. Just saying thank you will go a long way.

One tip for when you talk to the gatekeeper (or even the decision maker if you get through to them) is to avoid giving up too much information on the first call; save the good stuff for the in-person meeting. Let your gatekeeper know that you don't have a lot of time. Boldly let them know the decision maker wants to meet with you. Create a sense of urgency. If you get through to a potential decision maker, this applies also. Avoid discussions that should be reserved for face-to-face meetings; be a drinking fountain rather than a fire hose.

Sell only to the decision maker; don't waste your time pitching to someone without the authority or need. This will mean asking a lot of questions about them. Luckily, in the internet age, we can do much of our research before the call. Disqualify the buyers who cannot make a decision. That may prove to be a very high percentage of your calls, but your face-to face calls are reserved for selling. Research is done before you meet the decision maker and this can be done on the phone ahead of time.

Try to say the person's name as many times as possible in the call. This technique works because many buyers enjoy talking about themselves, since it is their favorite subject. Let's say the prospect is named Bob. The dialog could go something like this:

You: "Bob?"
Bob: "Yes."
You: "Bob?"
Bob: "Yes, this is Bob".
You: "Bob, let me introduce myself. I am JJ and was referred to you by Ken of AT&T. Bob?"
Bob: "Yes?"
You: "Bob, I am in the area tomorrow and I would like ten minutes of your time to discuss how to reduce your phone bill. Bob, I am available at 1:10 p.m. and or 1:20 PM. It will only take ten minutes unless you have questions. Bob?"
Bob: "Yes?"
You: "Which time is best for you, Bob?"
Bob: "1:10 p.m., if it is only ten minutes."
You: "Bob, that's great. See you tomorrow at 1:10 p.m."

In less than a minute, you have said Bob's name ten times, while Bob has said yes four times. Psychologically speaking, the conversation focused on him and we had him saying yes. This is an "old school" sales technique that works. It is good way to start a new relationship.

One thing that you may have also noticed in the example above is the novel way I set appointments with start times at ten-minute intervals and never at the hour or half hour. Why do this? It sets the tone for the meeting that what you have to offer is going to be different. If asked why the odd appointment time, suggest that your time is important and that you pride yourself in keeping a strict schedule. Give it a shot and I bet you will be pleased with the results. You will be remembered for this different approach to appointment scheduling.

You must try this: Schedule an hour on a Friday afternoon for calling to get appointments. (This is sometimes called a "call blitz".) Prepare a list of people to call. Limit the calls to just prospects. Call as many prospects as you can in the hour. Measure your success by the number of appointments received.

62. First Impressions Happen Only Once

"You can see a lot by just looking."

Yogi Berra (1935–) Professional baseball player

Psychologists believe that we can size up someone new in about three or four seconds (plus or minus a couple of seconds). We respond to visual cues such as the way someone dresses and how he or she grooms themselves. We do a quick check on body language. Our nose quickly verifies how someone smells. We listen to speech patterns. We assess their physical appearance head to toe. All this data translates into a first impression. Then the judgment is made. Go ahead now and try to change our minds after we have made this assessment.

We have already categorized this new person by one the following subcategories:

- The new person is like us and we like that.
- The new person is better than us, and that can be good or bad.
- The new person is not as good as us, and that can be good or bad.

If the new person is one of us, we will invite that new person into the tribe, the office, or the club. We feel comfortable with the new person and we will share our food, our thoughts, and our time. Bring out the welcome wagon; the prodigal son has returned.

If a new person is better than us, often we are suspicious; we want to know why this person is better and we wonder what they want from us. We may also desire to be with them socially since they have an advantage over us; maybe we can learn from them or maybe we can get some of what they have. Sometimes, we snub this person because we are envious and we feel inferior. We realize that they will never join our tribe, but we may offer anyway. We are envious of their status.

If a new person is not as good as us, we may tolerate them. Sometimes, we even like them because it feels good to be around them. We take pleasure in that we are superior while acknowledging that we may need what this person has or can do. However, they can never really join the club. They are not good enough. We use them.

Knowing that this type of evaluation occurs every time someone meets you in a new selling or a networking environment, I suggest that you think ahead. This may seem obvious, but remember your grooming and hygiene. Use good eye contact. Dress professionally but not flamboyantly. Use good posture. Be polite and don't say anything unusual. Smile, you're on Candid Camera!

Three to four seconds is over pretty quick.

One more thing: Next time that you meet someone for the first time, immediately say his or her first name (i.e., in the first three to four seconds). Say, "Sally, it is a pleasure to meet you". If you can, try to say their name five more times in the conversation that follows; it will help you remember their name and it will focus the conversation on them. Remember, it is all about them.

63. Have You Heard Any Unique Value Propositions Today?

"He who refuses to embrace a unique opportunity loses the prize as surely if he had failed."

William James (1842–1910) Philosopher

An over-used and abused phrase, a "unique value proposition" (UVP), is a statement that tells why someone should buy your product or solution; it summarizes the differentiating benefits of your product or solution for your customer. It is a selling statement. It is also known as positioning statement, a value proposition, and a selling proposition.

When you are out looking for money, venture capitalists like to ask you to recite your UVP. I like to ask VCs what they mean by that question and I find generally they cannot define it, but they know they need to ask that question. It is their job to ask smart questions. However, I digress.

I am not a fan of lengthy UVPs and I think that two sentences are typically enough. The first sentence should identify the target customer and the need for the product or solution. The second sentence should compare the product or solution to the current alternatives and describe what is unique about the new product or solution. The emphasis of the UVP should be on the benefits to the customer and not a recitation of product features or specifications. Benefits normally include intangibles such ease of use, convenience, speed, cost reduction, or status. A good UVP should make the customer ask more questions.

Critical to a good UVP is the understanding of what is truly valuable to the customer. This is not guess work, but is the result of intense testing and market research. You need to understand why the customer is willing choose your product over a competitor's. Qualitative research such as focus groups or in-person interviews can help answer why customers choose your solution and this can help you refine your UVP. Citing a study that you conducted that found that 63% of the people surveyed preferred your product or solution helps validate your claim. It will also make the venture capital guys happy.

Homework Assignment: Write a couple of paragraphs about the unique benefits that your firm offers. Play with the words and try to reduce it to just a couple of well-written, descriptive sentences. Share the final draft with others and ask for feedback; listen and make the modifications that they suggest. Voila! You have a UVP.

64. Decades: To Whom Are You Selling?

"I've learned that people will forget what you said, people will forget what you did, but people will never forget how you made them feel."

Maya Angelou (1928–) American poet

People sell to people and everyone is different. One factor that determines the differences in people is the decade when an individual comes of age. Psychologists have determined that people most often reach final emotional maturity in their early twenties; this parallels a solidification of their values. This maturation coincides with the witnessing of key events in their lives. These events could be cultural, historical, or personal, but in all cases, these events helped define the person who lived through them.

In fact, some experts feel that your values are solidified at an even earlier age. Dr. Morris Massey writes in WHAT YOU ARE IS WHERE YOU WERE WHEN that the average person's values get programmed into them at age ten! He calls it gut-level programming which means that our parents (or the lack of parenting) shape us more than we might like to admit. He hypothecates that our behaviors are a reflection of our values and that our values are shaped by significant events that are personal, cultural, or familial. He states that to figure out what is going on in a person's head, you need to look at what was happening to them when they were ten years old.

To generalize, people who mature at the same approximate time and witness similar major events in their lives can subdivided into subgroups by decade. Let's say that you turned twenty years old in 1985; for convenience, let's call you an 80's person. What major events would you have witnessed or experienced in that decade? I can name a few: the assassination of John Lennon, the Challenger disaster, the Reagan Era, the fall of Berlin Wall, Madonna, Yuppies, and the movie ET. We can argue over who was more significant (Reagan or Madonna?), but, clearly, some unique things happened during that decade that have left a lasting imprint on the lives of the people that came of age in the eighties.

Eighties people are unique because of what they did and did not experience. It was a time of relative economic prosperity and an absence of war. A new conservative culture emerged that supported Reagan's conservative agenda; young people traded in their disco clothes for golf shirts and penny loafers and called themselves yuppies. The Soviet Union crumbled and capitalism won. Thus, these events helped shape the values of people who came of age that time, along with personal events unique to each such as living in a home with just one parent, etc.

When selling to an eighties person it is important to understand that they may view the world differently than you. This requires sensitivity on your part to avoid saying the wrong things; you need to put yourself in their shoes. For example, I am a seventies person and during much of my career I have sold to sixties people. (The more I learn about the sixties, the more I wish had experienced more of that period, by the way.) I have found the Vietnam experience to be an event of galactic proportions to the sixties decade group. It seems that there were two subgroups: one that supported the war and may have done a tour of duty in Vietnam; and, the other, which was fiercely anti-war and may have participated in protest marches. Talk about an explosive issue.

What I have learned is that the people who experienced this crucial period in history remain highly opinionated about it. Scratch the surface on this issue and you will find strong opinions. Take the wrong side and you can become an enemy and it becomes the sixties all over again. My advice is to proceed with caution, if not avoid the topic altogether. You need to know and anticipate who you are selling to and what not to say.

Being "neutral" as a salesperson is critical; most successful sales-people are chameleon-like with an ability to adapt to different people and cultures. When selling to someone from a different age group or decade, think before you speak and try to understand what he or she might have experienced. Avoid the pitfall of putting your foot in your mouth with a statement or opinion that shuts down your prospect.

The advertising world likes to categorize us by generation: the Baby Boomers (born 1946–1964, Generation X (1965–1979), and the Millenni-als (1980–2000). For me these time frames are just too big. Even a decade view can be sweeping. Additionally, segmenting customers by decade is not the only way to segment your customer. Race, ethnicity, wealth, geog-raphy, and income are a few of the others. The overriding point is that peo-ple are different and we need to market and sell to them accordingly.

Below are some significant events listed by decade. Can you think of other cultural or historical events that may define people by their decade?

The 50's

- Ike
- McCarthyism
- The Mickey Mouse Club

- Roy Rogers
- Elvis
- Leave it to Beaver

The 60s

- JFK assassination
- MLK assassination
- Vietnam War
- Woodstock
- Easy Rider
- Man walks on the moon
- The Beatles

The 70's

- Nixon and Watergate
- ET and Star Wars
- Streaking
- Disco
- Hostage crisis in Iran
- Women's movement

The 80s

- Reagan
- Berlin Wall falls
- Communism gasps a last breath
- Challenger disaster
- Assassination of John Lennon
- The personal computer
- Punk rock

The 90s

- Desert Storm
- Magic Johnson announced HIV positive
- Nirvana

- OJ Simpson trial
- Starbucks
- Clinton impeachment
- Rap music goes mainstream
- Dotcom
- The internet

The 2000's

- Sept 11
- Terrorism
- iPods
- Cell phones everywhere
- Iraq War
- More to come

Try this: Next time that you are on a sales call, guess which decade your customer is from. Think about what they may have experienced or lived through.

65. *Retaining Top Sales Talent*

"We're adding a little something to this month's sales contest. As you all know, first prize is a Cadillac El Dorado. Anybody want to see second prize? Second prize is a set of steak knives. Third prize is you're fired."

From the movie Glengarry Glen Ross (1992)

An entrepreneur's worst nightmare may be the surprise resignation of a top sales rep. It is unfortunately a common practice when managing high-achieving sales reps to let them sell and stay out of their way. The problem with this mind-set is that we think that they are happy. This may not be the case and the opposite may be true. Many times top sales talent need to be fed continuous praise and new challenges; if they don't get this feedback, they leave.

It is my estimation that top sales reps leave for many reasons including the following:

- Desire for new challenges, personal growth, and advancement
- Increased work loads and expectations with declining rewards
- Poor management or conflicts with management
- Unresolved grievances
- Feeling disconnected from the company vision, mission, and strategy
- Broken promises and a loss of trust
- Too many changes to their accounts, territory, and compensation plans
- More money offered another employer; this is often cited as the number one reason for leaving
- Personal needs not being met

The cost of recruiting, hiring, and training a new rep can be staggering; depending on your industry, the costs run into the tens of thousands of dollars. I have seen estimates that exceed six figures after only a year. Meanwhile, you are waiting for payback on your investment.

The cost of losing a top rep can be substantial. Depending on the industry, the departing rep might try to take his clients with him to the new firm; this can be devastating and could take months or years to repair, if at all. Additionally, while still working at his old employer, the rep's productivity may severely decline, while doing a job search. After the rep leaves, your customers are impacted with an interruption of service. No matter how you cut it, your image is tarnished when a top rep leaves. If it happens often, your firm looks plain silly.

Flight risk should be formally reviewed on an annual basis and more often in vulnerable periods such as when competitors are making a hard push in your backyard. Look for warning signs. Reps with significant longevity automatically qualify as candidates for high flight risk; for this type of rep, the challenge is to keep on going and minimize boredom.

Retaining top reps is not complex, but it may require the entrepreneur to adjust sales management style and process. First, make sure that the top sales reps have the opportunity and the forum to share their ideas. Management needs to listen and solicit input from the rep. The process of sharing ideas might be therapeutic for the rep but you will likely learn a lot.

Top reps tend to be strategic and this carries over to how they manage their careers and their needs for personal and career development. Entrepreneurs need to understand the goals of the reps and provide a path at the firm for the reps to get what they want for their career. This accommodation can ensure the reps will stay; conversely, with no plan to help the reps grow and learn, the reps will likely leave. You must communicate a genuine concern for the reps' future.

Mentoring provides a great opportunity for a senior rep to grow, while helping a new sales rep learn the business. This process happens naturally and informally in most organizations, so go ahead and sponsor it. Consider letting the senior rep mentor a junior rep; provide the senior rep with additional compensation in the form of a bonus or override; be specific about how long the formal mentoring period will last, such as six months. The bond created with the senior rep and the junior rep will likely outlive the special payout, and the payoff to the firm can be substantial. The payout to the senior rep does not have to be substantial, while its benefits will be.

We know that reps may leave for more money when courted by another firm. There may be other root issues, but money talks. My suggestion is to pay them more money. Pay them enough to keep them on board, since we know that the replacement cost can be staggering, if debilitating to the firm. I have seen too many top reps leave when a small increase in pay could have averted the whole matter. This can include bonuses, special commissions, stock, perks such as a car plan, or a richer expense account. It is just that simple.

I am sure that you have heard about the "Pareto Principle", also known as the "80/20 Rule", which claims that that 80% of all sales are made by 20% of the salespeople. This may describe the top sales reps at most of the firms that I have worked at and maybe at your firm too. These reps are as good as gold and you have got to keep them on the team. Don't think twice. Pay them what they need and then maybe a little more. Trust me. You will sleep better at night.

Top sales reps need to feel recognized and appreciated. While money is important, recognition is powerful and simple to give. Say thanks at company meetings, praise them in writing, and recognize their efforts on a day-to-day basis. Many entrepreneurs think that good sales management is providing constructive criticism; while this is true, you need to send positive, affirming messages with far greater frequency.

Phil Jackson, celebrated coach of the Los Angeles Lakers professional basketball team, manages world-class athletes who make millions of dollars and who have fame that most of us will never know. Still, Jackson believes that he must provide five positive messages for each constructive criticism given to an individual player. It sounds easy, but it is not. I recommend that you keep a score sheet of your praise and criticism for your top reps. See if you can coach like Phil Jackson. He seems to do it right.

For some people, personal priorities make the difference between leaving and staying. Sales reps will choose to stay with a firm that understands their special needs such working from home, flexible hours, and extra time off. Dual career families can have special needs that can be accommodated by the firm. Entrepreneurs can provide the special accommodations that can be the difference in keeping top talent.

An important factor for retention of top talent can be the quality or effectiveness of the immediate management. Effective managers should communicate openly, listen with intention, set clear performance expectations, and give feedback. They need to speak the language of the sales rep. Nothing is more frustrating to salespeople than when the boss does not "get it"; without the day-to-day contact of the customer, the boss loses touch with the market and relies on memories of what worked before. More than anything else, the boss needs to listen.

Finally, retention must be an on-going priority and should be a daily task, rather than a reactive attempt to reverse surprise resignations.

Must do list: Take your top rep (and spouse) out to dinner; express your thanks for all the hard work. Say thank you in front of the spouse.

66. *Hiring Top Sales Talent from the Competition*

"Nudge, nudge, wink, wink. Know what I mean?"

Monty Python's Flying Circus (1969–1974) Comedy troupe

Finding the right sales talent to join your firm is a major challenge and it can be very tempting to recruit potential employees from your competition. They know the industry, they are trained or trainable, and they should easily transition into your organization. Sales reps at the competition can be particularly interesting recruits, since they might bring customer relationships with them and help you expand your market share. This may be true, but I suggest that you move with caution.

The first thing I recommend is that you research the competitor's history with former employees. Has there been litigation, or threats of lawsuits by the company against former employees that have left to go to another competing firm? In this case, it would be wise to know your enemy before you make an offer.

If you are interviewing someone from the competition, make sure you get to review all their employment agreements that include language regarding non-compete, non-solicitation of employees, non-solicitation of customers, and confidentiality. This should be reviewed by your attorney before an offer is made to determine if limitations exist; note that state employment laws vary significantly, with California known as the most the employee friendly. What works in New York might send you to court in Los Angeles.

As with any new hire, an assessment of the prospective rep's fit with your company culture is paramount. No matter how good the rep might be, if he or she does "fit in" with your culture, you will have problems sooner or later. The appeal of the potential big producer is a siren's song, but it is not worth compromising your ethics or values. Slow down and be sure to background check the potential new hire. I recommend having multiple team members interview the candidate; consistency is a significant attribute in a sales rep.

If you proceed with an offer, make sure that the offer letter specifically prohibits the new employee from disclosing his previous employer's trade secrets or confidential information. Secrets will do you no good and you don't want to hear about them. Tell the new employee verbally and in writing.

Before the new employee starts, remind the employee not to preannounce the job change to customers. Instead, your company will announce the arrival of the new employee. Also, inform the new employee not to copy the former company's records, contact databases, or files. Explicitly state that this is not acceptable behavior and that you do not want this information. By the way, if the new employee downloads contact information from Lotus Notes or Outlook, it is easily traceable by the guys in the IT department at the former employee. A prosecuting attorney would refer to this as "evidence".

When a rep from the competition is hired, it is often presumed that the rep's former customers will follow. In practice, this can prove very awkward for the customer and the rep. You need to look at the situation from the customer perspective. On Monday, the rep is selling for Firm A pitching their great products; then on Tuesday the same rep is now selling for Firm B saying how great Firm B's products are. What is the customer to believe?

At your firm, the new rep joins the team, but your employees keep thinking of the new rep as from the competition. This is an awkward adjustment for all parties, which needs to be considered before hand. You can hire from the competition, but be very careful to do so in an ethical and legal manner. See your attorney before you hire that superstar sales rep from your competitor.

Go ahead and talk: When a sales rep from a competitor calls, invite the rep to lunch. It is good to dine with the enemy; you may get a lot of competitive intelligence and you may get to meet your new top sales rep.

67. How Do I Set Up a Website? (Skip This If You Have One Already)

"I saw the angel in the marble and carved until I set him free."

Michelangelo (1475–1564) Artist

Depending on your computer skills, the time available, and the size of your money tree, here are some options on building a website.

- Hire a consultant to do the work for you. The consultant, often called a web designer, can customize a website to meet your specifications. The price range for this work can vary depending on the consultant's design fee rates, the time involved, and the tools used. Most beginning sites can be created for below a $1,000. Large commercial sites can cost much more.
- Alternatively, you can buy a website software package and do it yourself. Using "templates" software, a novice can design a website for about $200. Using this approach, you fill in the blanks with your content. The downside is that you will have little design flexibility and you should be prepared to see your same design elsewhere on the internet.
- If you have the time and the computer skills, you can create your own website. You will have to master a development tool like Microsoft FrontPage; for most of us, this is really not a prudent option.

Besides the design and the content development (which is the hard part), you will need a domain name such as www.firstbestordifferent.com. Enter the words "domain name" in Google and you will find thousands of sources of domain names. The challenge will be to find a good domain name that is available. Most businesses will want a ".com" domain name and you will be stunned to find that seemingly every name has already been taken by someone else. Be prepared to invest some time on this search and be prepared to let go of that perfect domain name that you started with since it won't be available.

You also will need a web-hosting firm to store your site on their server. The website host will provide a gateway to the internet, along with a backup process to ensure that your hard work on your website won't get lost when their system crashes. I recommend that you seek a referral from someone you know that has a website host that they are pleased with; most of these hosting firms are small shops.

To do list: Start visiting websites and review them with a critical eye. Which ones are easy to navigate? Where are the buttons to get more infor-mation? Can you find the information that you want? Is the content up to date?

68. *What is the Purpose of Your Website?*

"To forget one's purpose is the commonest form of stupidity."

Friedrich Nietzsche (1844–1900) German philosopher

Websites have many purposes.

Entertainment is a common purpose of many websites. On this type of website, content is king and needs to be frequently updated to keep your audience coming back for more.

Many websites exist to sell something to the visitor directly online. Ease of use is critical for this website. Visitors need to be able to navigate to the product or solution quickly, get necessary product information, and easily make the purchase. Sounds easy, but it can be hard to do. Large product lines that are purchased by a diverse customer base can create complexity. Additionally, the customer must be confident that the website transaction is secure; if not, the customer will just leave.

Some websites help the visitor solve problems. Driven by a need to fix a problem or learn something, this visitor is motivated by pain or need and is often very impatient. This visitor might be quicker to buy a solution. Layout of the home page is critical for this visitor; they need to be able find what they need quickly. Time is running out.

Visitors can come to a website for information. Downloads, newsletters, alerts, and blogs help give the visitor what they want. Obtaining this desired information can be a necessary step in the "pre-purchase due diligence" that some buyers must do. Some visitors may have to visit a website many times before they are comfortable in making a purchase decision.

A website can help the entrepreneur save money since it can be less expensive than printing on paper; additionally the distribution costs are minimal when compared to bulk mail. Updates can be made easily and there is no waste of printed materials when a change is made. Websites can create leads for the small business. By having the visitor register at the website, prospect name development is created or maintained. The visitor can also request to be contacted or to be sent samples.

When designing your website, first determine what the purpose of the website will be; this will help dictate design and content decisions.

Answer these questions: What is the purpose of your website? Is your current website designed to do that? If not, you better change it.

69. The "Must-Have" List for Your Website

"The most important thing in communication is to hear what is being said."

Peter Drucker (1909–2005) Organizational theorist

A good website must have the following features and elements:

- A banner across the top of the home page can add a graphical element to display your company name, logo and tagline.
- It must load quickly on the average PC. Websites with exploding fireworks, dogs barking, and sirens blaring seldom do much more than waste your visitors' valuable time. More typically, when a website requires too much time to load because of a flashy, memory intensive-design, the visitor will choose to click on to the next website. They won't come back to your site again.
- Your contact information must be on the home page, since some visitors will want to contact you now but won't bother to search your website for this information.
- Your website should have an "About Us" section, which explains to the visitor who you are.
- If you want to sell stuff on the internet, make it easy to do so. Place a button in clear view so the visitor can order; don't make the visitor hunt for your shopping cart. This also applies to product information; make it easy for the visitor to find the product description or specifications.
- Have a button that allows your visitor to register if they are new or to sign in if they are a returning visitor.
- Although there are many options for the location of the buttons and links on your home page, the most common practice is to locate them on the left side of the page.
- Have the date last edited displayed on the home page so that your visitor will know that you keep your pages updated.
- Each page needs a title that states the contents of the page. When people click through a website, it is possible to become lost or to become disoriented. Make it easy for people to navigate by letting them know where they are.
- Be sure to include a copyright statement at the bottom of each page to let folks know that this is your original work.

- List links of favorite sites and affiliates. This is a common practice on the internet. By linking to other sites, it will provide value to your visitors and it will create an opportunity for Google to find your site by linking to sites that they have already identified. When a partner website lists your link, this is called a reciprocal link.
- To keep the visitor coming back, you need to keep the website updated with new meaningful and useful content. Weekly updates are a must and daily might be better. Yep, this is a big commitment.
- Writing for the web is a critical element of your website's success. If you are not a strong writer, then consider a professional copywriter.
- The layout of headers and body copy needs to be carefully thought out to help the reader find the relevant information. I like lots of white space to isolate important information; conversely, I am turned off by websites that are too busy.
- Photos and quality graphics can help communicate better than words.
- People love free stuff. People will spend more time on your site if they are going to get something for free, even if it's a simple download of some generic professional advice on how to do something better.

Schedule this for Friday afternoon: Audit your website for all the "must-have features" in this chapter; if you don't have them all, consider making the changes now.

70. *How to Create Website Traffic*

"Americans will put up with anything provided it doesn't block traffic".

Dan Rather (1931–) News anchor

After your website is up and running, the primary objective is getting people to visit it. There are a number of methods to drive the "hits" on your website:

- Content is everything. Inform your visitors, help them solve a problem or entertain them. Give them a reason to come back. I cannot emphasize enough the sheer importance of content. A website with meaningful content offers a terrific opportunity for establishing yourself as an authority on your business, or as I like to call it, a knowledge broker.
- The use of advertising is a common method to encourage people to visit a website. Your print media advertisements should always include your website address. Often the secondary purpose of an ad campaign (after brand awareness) is to encourage people to go to the website for more information. Every printed business communication should include the web address plainly visible; this includes business cards, letterhead, invoices, brochures, window signs, fax cover sheets, vehicle signs, media kits, yellow pages, surveys, radio advertising, and TV advertising. You cannot communicate your website address enough to your prospective customers.
- Consider the use of e-mail newsletters. This newsletter should go to friends of the website who have registered and have given permission for you to send them information. Depending on the business, a quarterly newsletter may the best choice; if you mail this newsletter too frequently, you are just spam and your message will be deleted. When you do send an e-mail newsletter, pack it with well-written, useful information. A good newsletter can create instant hits to your website; meanwhile, you are building or maintaining share of mind with the customer. Writing good e-mail newsletters can be challenging, so consider delegating the task to a journalist who has the time and the writing skills; meanwhile, you can function as editor and publisher. Starving college students, stay-at-home moms, and retirees are good outsourcing partners for this activity.

- Direct mailing (i.e., snail-mail) your newsletter to your customers is another way to encourage website visitors. This newsletter should have the same content as above, but it is delivered via another channel. Using multiple channels to deliver your message is sometimes called cross-channel marketing.
- Press releases are another great way to create visitors for your website. Your "news" may trigger the need for more information and a visit to your website. Encourage the press release reader to visit your website for more information on the topic covered in the press release. Make sure you direct the reader exactly where to go on your website. Nothing is more frustrating for visitors than searching a website and not finding what they wanted.
- The use of partners or affiliates is another simple but effective way to create traffic at your site. This can be as simple as another website displaying a link to your website; this link could be listed under a tab called "favorite links". Typically, you will offer the same courtesy to the other website by listing them under your favorite links.
- Direct mailing postcards can be an extremely effective tool for creating website traffic. See the chapter called "Direct Marketing with Postcards."
- "Search Engine Optimization" (also know as SEO) can mean many things, but the most important method to optimize a search for your website may be with Google AdWords. Some say that if you don't show up on a Google search, you don't exist. Is it that important? It can be a must do, if you're marketing a product or a solution that people prefer to find with the web. For a commodity product, it can mean the difference between success and failure. On the other hand, if your customer will be finding your site by directly entering your URL, search engine optimization may be less important. I read recently that over 80% of searches are now done by a search engine, rather than entering a specific URL. I understand that this percentage may be increasing.
- Meta Tags are usually located near the top of the page of most HTML files; they tell search engines to list your site in their indexes. They can also send some search engines to your website. Today, not all search engines look for Meta Tags; but it remains an important issue since some do.
- See the chapter called "Create More Website Traffic with Google AdWords."

One more thing: When someone visits your site, ask them how they heard about you?

71. Google AdWords Help People Find Your Website

"I think it's wrong that only one company makes the game Monopoly."

Steven Wright (1955–) Comedian

It is estimated that Google represents 75% of all search traffic world-wide. There are many search engines out there, but all pale in comparison to Google. In fact, a cottage industry has emerged of consultants who help firms identify the right AdWords for a website so that you can maximize traffic.

AdWords help narrow a search so that a customer can find your website. The factors that target your customer include language spoken, geography, the name of your solution, and keywords that describe your product or solution. Keywords are the words that most frequently appear on websites that describe solutions like yours. One good way to determine your keywords is to visit your competitors' websites to see what words are used to describe their business or solution. Compare that list with the keywords that you think best describe what you do. Each time that Google directs a customer to your site and they click on the site you get charged. Thus, selecting the right key words is critical to creating site activity. The number of clicks you get then determines the cost paid to Google. Google allows you to determine your budget for these costs. What a bunch of great folks!

Here are a few suggestions on getting started: Identify specific target phrases rather than generic terms. By using product or industry specific terms, you can narrow your search to your target market. If you use generic key words, the cost to you can be substantial and the quality of your leads can be suspect. After determining key phrases, you can then create your ad for Google. With this done, Google puts your ad up immediately and you are in business.

Next, watch your ad's metrics closely. When you first create a Google Ad, it is important to monitor its success and adjust it accordingly. This can save you money and create better leads. Google ranks keyword ads. The higher value searches get listed first. Some experts will tell you that you must be listed on the first two pages of a Google search or you won't be found in 95% of searches.

Everyone wants to be ranked number one on a Google Search and some firms will pay big money to make that happen. Interestingly enough, recent studies indicate that it may be better to be ranked two through four. For some reason, the visitor on a search will be more likely to scroll down to the middle of the page and click. Try to stay ranked two through four on the first page. You will need to audit this ranking periodically, since Google is a living software program and always changing.

To learn more go to https://adwords.google.com. You have got to do this if you are going to "play the game" on the internet.

When you have a minute: Create a list of the words or phrases that first come to mind about your business or solution. Look at the words or phrases used by other businesses. Enter them in Google and see who pops up.

72. Getting Listed on Google, Yahoo!, and MSN

"He's not pining, he's passed on. This parrot is no more. He has ceased to be. He's expired and gone to meet his maker. He's a stiff, bereft of life. He rests in peace. If you hadn't have nailed him to the perch he'd be pushing up the daisies. He's rung down the curtain and joined the choir invisible. This is an ex-parrot!"

Monty Python's Flying Circus (1969–1974) Comedy troupe

There are many search engines on the web (and few dead parrots), but the three that really count are Google, Yahoo!, and MSN; most of the other search engines pull their data from the big three and then value-add on top of them with special search features. Go with Google, Yahoo!, and MSN. Some topics and some industries have dedicated search engines; this chapter will focus on the big three only.

It is getting harder and harder to get listed on Google since they have determined that the web searcher wants answers and not thousands of old websites. To improve this search experience, they are screening out the "content poor" websites, such as websites that are old or that have a low page count. Google is fully automated and uses spiders, which are like software robots crawling all over the internet. No human editors are involved. They find your website via links to other websites that are on the directories. To appeal to Google, you need to continually refresh your website content; the more value you provide the visitor, the more likely you will get listed by Google.

You can also advertise on Google and pay to get listed; these are the ads on the right side of the Google page. You can submit your site (your URL) by going to Google's "Add URL"; approval can take a long time and there are no guarantees that they will actually approve it. The best way to ensure that you get on Google is to link your site with as many other sites as possible; almost by default, you get listed.

To get on MSN, go to http://search.msn.com/docs/submit.aspx. Be patient since the application process can be lengthy. Linking your way in proves a better route for most new sites. Do not keep re-submitting your site. It will not speed up the process of getting listed and may even get you banished from MSN.

For Yahoo!, the same linking in option is most commonly used.

Yahoo! maintains a category-based directory, which you can formally apply. Go to http://dir.yahoo.com

Stuff to do: Visit the three major search engines and familiarize yourself with them. Act like a web surfer who does not know about your firm. Search for your product or solution.

73. Have You Tried a Webinar Yet?

"Do, or do not. There is no try."

Yoda, from the movie THE EMPIRE STRIKES BACK (1980)

Webinars are an effective, low-cost way to sell your products. Webinars are "virtual meetings" that use the internet, the phone, and a Power-Point presentation. This type of presentation can be particularly effective with business-to-business sales efforts where your prospect is a busy executive. They can be great for launching new products, doing training sessions for new clients, and for selling to clients who are unfamiliar with your services. Kind of like a giant conference call, you can present to multiple prospects all over the state, the nation, or the world. Webinars can be very cost effective when you calculate the expenses that you normally incur with an in-person seminar and don't incur with a webinar: travel, presentation facility, hotel, and food.

To get started you will need a presentation, which is typically done in PowerPoint. Try to keep the presentation simple with minimal graphics, since you want the average viewer to be able to be able to quickly download the content on their PC. Complex images and fancy graphics could slow the start of the meeting or make it next to impossible for someone with an older PC to participate. Additionally, viewers who cannot quickly load the content will become impatient and will just drop off the line.

After that, you will need to choose a webinar provider. You will find that there are many available. Go to Google and enter the word "webinar"; you will be stunned at the options available. Some will charge by the attendee, by the month, by the hour, by the minute, or by flat fees. The webinar provider will provide a website for you and your attendees to navigate to, along with passwords, login information, and an 800 dial-in phone number.

Your presentation can be set up to be a one-way communication with you as a "talking head", or better yet, it can be interactive. Generally, webinar providers allow the customer to ask questions over the phone or ask questions via a chat line. A few things to think about before you launch your first webinar:

- Do a dry run with your webinar service. Make sure that you understand the dynamics of presenting to a virtual audience and understand how to manage the technology. Have your staff and friends critique your first efforts.

- Practice your presentation ahead of time; a good speech is one that is rehearsed many times before it is finally given. The best webinar service cannot make up for a lousy presentation.
- Announce a start time and stick to it. People are busy and you don't want to waste their time with delays or idle banter. Don't let an audience member interrupt you while you are presenting; mute features are available and may be useful. One way to manage distractions is to announce at the beginning that the "mute switch" will be engaged during the presentation, but will be turned off at the end for questions and answers.
- If any special technology issues need to be addressed, such as lengthy downloads or unique security requirements, advise your customers ahead of time. Request that they sign in early to get this completed.
- You might want to ask your customers to prepare questions for the "Q and A" session at the end of the formal presentation. By holding the questions to the end, you can get to the main points of the presentation and not lose your train of thought. Consider having canned questions planted with participating staff members so the question and answer session gets off to a good start.
- End the session with a call to action for your customers. Tell them what to do next. For example, you might want to offer a landing page for them to visit for more information. Or, you could direct them to your website store to order the product.

Consider archiving the presentation for future use on your website. This could be used by other customers or could be used as a training tool for future employees.

A thing to try: If you have not participated in a webinar lately or ever, sign up for one and see what it is like being a prospect on the phone looking at a PowerPoint.

74. Have You Heard About Podcasting?

"There is no reason anyone would want a computer in their home."

Ken Olson (1926–) Chairman and founder of Digital Equipment Corporation

Podcasting is named after the iPod, Apple's portable MP3 player. Podcasting allows the end-user to download electronic files from the internet onto a MP3 player or PC; the content publisher gives end-users updates using a RSS (Rich Site Summary) feed. The content publisher or "podcaster" produces multimedia (audio and video) files in MP3 format (There are other formats by the way.) and publishes this information online for the end-user. Almost any type of content can be published in this format including talk shows, technical manuals, music, books, and others, which is the charm of it all. The software to do this is free which allows anyone with a website to be a podcaster.

An end-user does not need an iPod or MP3 player; in fact, most podcasts are listened to on a PC. You may hear podcasting with video files referred to as "video podcasting" or other names. Regardless of the names, the principal is the same; compare it to a pre-recorded TV or radio program. The updates to a podcast are like episodes of a TV series; the different episodes can be stored on a MP3 player or on your PC for future use. (Yes, these are reruns!).

For the small business, a podcast is another way to communicate intimately with your customers. Some podcast content is very slick and has radio or TV production qualities while other podcasts feel as if they are homemade. Podcasts create intimacy because of the emotional content that an audio file can offer over a PowerPoint, a web page, or a paper brochure. For the entrepreneur who routinely communicates to his customers, a podcast can be an excellent, low-cost way to get a message out.

A financial planning firm would be a good example of an application for podcasting; with the rules for investment planning constantly changing, the financial planner can record an episode or an update as frequently as needed. This can be made available on the website for the end-user. Other businesses that might want to consider podcasting are CPA firms, law practices, and other service providers. A firm that has routine technical updates to its product line might want to use podcasts.

As I write this, podcasts are a hot trend and have a special cachet. Give it a try.

Try something new: I would guess that you have not listened to a podcast. Give it a try. Visualize yourself as the speaker talking about your business.

75. What the Heck is Blogging?

"Trends, like horses, are easier to ride in the direction they are going."

John Naisbitt (1929–) Businessman

Blogging? Sounds like a Scandinavian dance done with wooden shoes to me.

Blogging has actually been around since the early 1990's and the early days of the web. Simply described, blogging is an internet journal that is frequently updated and usually written in the first person. With readily available software and linking websites, anybody with a keyboard and the time can blog.

Sometimes, blogs or weblogs are written just for family or friends; others are very topic specific and niche focused. Controversy has been common with blogs since there has been so little protocol or self-regulation. Let's just say, names get named in blogs. Some blogs have been outright libelous and the courts are learning about them. They can provide an amazing forum for political commentary and free speech.

However, the ones we hear about in the business press are diaries written on products and services for public consumption. They can be major media instruments spinning products and services with instant access to the readership or customer. You can think of them like a newspaper column, but without the editorial restriction, rules, or objectivity. A weblog is essentially a journal on a website that is updated often and allows the readers access to the journal entries. Many weblogs allow the readers to respond, thus making the process interactive. One weblog entry can receive hundreds of responses, depending on the size of your readership. Talk about creating a buzz! It can be instantaneous.

An internet file format called RSS (Rich Site Summary) is commonly used and allows anyone with a website to distribute their content via syndication. Distributed excerpts tease the reader, while links allow the reader direct access to the blog website. One blog search engine called Technorati uses RSS to track and update excerpts for millions of blogs.

Blogging can be very efficient when compared to doing traditional updates on your website; the software is readily available from websites like blogger.com. You can do it yourself and you don't have to call the web designer; it is just as easy as writing an e-mail. Blogs are not a substitute for a website since the customer still needs somewhere to go to find out more about the company or solution.

Business can use a weblog as a promotional tool, which can build brand awareness. For many firms, being positioned as a knowledge broker is an effective way to self promote. Blogging is the perfect vehicle for a knowledge broker. Blogs can allow direct communication to customers and prospects while sharing knowledge and expertise.

Before deciding to set up weblog, give some thought to what you want to accomplish with a blog. Blog on, dude.

Get started: Start reading blogs on subjects of interest; get a feel for the type of content that can appear in a blog. Next, download the blog software. Begin blogging.

76. Wiki! Wiki!

"The crowd makes the ball game."

Ty Cobb (1886–1961) Baseball player

Wiki! Wiki! is Hawaiian for "hurry quickly" or "hurry, hurry". This phrase is not to be confused with a "wiki", which is a type of website (actually a type of software) that allows the visitor or reader to easily make edits, deletes, and contributions to content on a website. The easy-to-use software helps the visitor make these changes without having to know how to write in HTML code, which is the computer language used by web designers.

The best-known example of a wiki is the free online encyclopedia WIKIPEDIA, which has taken the web by storm. WIKIPEDIA is a collaborative depository of information with a virtual authorship. It is self-regulating and is constantly being updated.

Wikis can be used for "internal consumption only" at large organizations. A large corporation could use a wiki as a "virtual blackboard"; this wiki would function as a tool to document a discussion about a new strategy or change that involves a complex process and lots of people. In this environment, the wiki facilitates the change and allows all employees to join in and have their say about the future.

Wikis can also be completely public in nature. Informal groups of people with common interests are forming wikis to collaborate and to share information and ideas. Wikis can be used for entertainment purposes such as a giant joke depository and exchange. Companies, consortiums, industry associations, and just about any online community can collaborate with a wiki. Maybe one of the best examples of wiki usage is at universities; educators and students have embraced wikis for "distance learning" which are virtual classrooms that allow students to collaborate from remote locations.

The software industry has embraced a wiki methodology known as "open source" for a number of years. New software has been written and then pre-released via open source websites. Software developers and end-users evaluated the new software and helped debug it (find problems or errors). The prevailing philosophy behind open source is that there is wisdom in crowds. Essentially, a single software engineer can write an innovative piece of software, but it takes hundreds or thousands of engineers to debug it. By making the software free and available, the software is spread in a viral nature. Some believe that this open source process can be applied to almost anything from science to literature to marketing.

Wikis are everywhere and easy to find. Wiki links are proudly displayed on corporation websites. Many wikis are linked to other wikis. There are websites that function as wiki directories allowing you find wikis that speak to your personal interest and there are wiki sites dedicated to the creation of new wikis. Domain names are also now available as ".wiki".

For an entrepreneur, wikis can be a superb promotional vehicle; many wikis allow "by-lines" which identify you as the contributor of new information or of an article. This can help you present yourself as being expert in a particular subject; I like to call this being a knowledge broker. An example of this would be a wiki that is dedicated to a common problem shared by a purchasing group; as a vendor that provides solutions in this area, you can register your firm as a provider. This could include contact information and product descriptions. Of course, your entry would be subject to the regulatory practices of the wiki and could be later edited or deleted.

It is easy to envision a time in the future when user groups could exist for any major product or service; to be a player or to be a qualified vendor, a firm's offering would need to be first evaluated and possibly tested by the virtual community. Wikis could play both an incredible check and balance for the end-customer and a new channel of distribution for the provider.

Wikis can promote or denigrate a brand. Like public relations, there are few controls over wikis. Wikis can function like viral marketing in that an idea can be quickly communicated to the online readership; since wikis are self-regulating, they can also be subject to manipulation. Thus, a wiki's content is only as reliable as is its readership. A product or solution can be praised or ridiculed on a wiki site; it is up to the wiki community to responsibly regulate themselves.

As I write this book, it looks as if wikis will have significant impact on the way people share and use information; I strongly suggest that you monitor this new online trend. Better yet, dive in and commit yourself to learning about wikis.

How about this? Go check out WIKIPEDIA. I bet you will never use your old encyclopedia again.

77. Internet Article Marketing Builds Instant Awareness for You and Your Website

"To market, to market, to buy a fat pig,
Home again, home again, dancing a jig;
To market, to market, to buy a fat hog;
Home again, home again, jiggety-jog;
To market, to market, to buy a plum bun,
Home again, home again, market is done."

Mother Goose Rhymes (1780)

One of the better ways to promote your business instantly on the web is article marketing. Article marketing is simply defined as writing short, content-rich articles for distribution on the web by third-party online publishers or "e-zines". Some of these magazines on the web have massive subscriber lists, while other e-zines depend on visitors searching a specific topic to find your article. The desired result for you as the author is the same as getting quoted in the newspaper: you get free publicity and your hope is for people to hit your website link for more information.

As a knowledge broker, it is your role to provide help to others with the article; thus, the article needs to have substance and be actionable. Rather than a press release or a fluff piece, you need to offer actionable information to your reader. Don't sell and don't close in your article. The mission is to help your reader to better understand a problem or an issue, while subtlety presenting you as an expert. The plan is to get them to buy later.

Know that the information offered will be downloaded and copied, since most people feel that whatever they find on the web is "finders keepers". Rather than battling to protect your copyright, focus your energy on creating a new relationship with the reader. You need to convince them to go to your website and save it as one of their favorites. Of course, your mission is to get them to contact you directly to discuss your products and services. It first starts with delivering value in your article.

You can submit your article to "article submission" websites, which are third parties that will provide your article to the online publishers, or you can contact the e-zines directly. Google actually ranks the submission websites by volume of activity using a tool called PageRank, which calculates a PR score. Focus on the submission websites with high scores. For more information on this, visit Google and enter the key word PageRank. Be sure to begin this process by already being linked with as many other websites as possible. One way that you get found by Google is to have existing live links with other websites and directories. Remember most readers find you because of their key word searches and the search engines that find your article.

When you submit an article give it a catchy headline; your first goal is to get their attention, so it is OK to be a little sensational or outrageous. Also, repeat your keywords through out the article, since you are writing for the internet and you want to be found by the search engine spiders. The electronic article submission form includes a resource box placed at the end of your article that allows your article to be linked back to your site.

These articles have a long life on the web and it may take many weeks and sometimes months before you receive the benefits of your article. Often your article will be archived on the publisher's website; it could be there for years. Write numerous articles, since your visitor will be more likely to visit your website if they start seeing your name with frequency.

Idea: Go to PageRank and check out article submission sites that cover your niche.

78. *Spam, Spam, Spam, Spam*

"Well, there's egg and bacon; egg, sausage and bacon; egg and SPAM;
bacon and SPAM; egg, bacon, sausage and SPAM; SPAM, bacon,
sausage and SPAM; SPAM, egg, SPAM, SPAM, bacon and SPAM;
SPAM, SPAM, SPAM, egg and SPAM; SPAM, SPAM, SPAM, SPAM,
SPAM, SPAM, baked beans, SPAM, SPAM, SPAM and SPAM; or
Lobster Thermidor aux crevettes with a Mornay sauce garnished with
truffle paté, brandy and a fried egg on top of SPAM."

Monty Python's Flying Circus (1969–1974) Comedy troupe

My apologies to Monty Python, but spam is not a laughing matter.

On January 1, 2004, the CAN-SPAM Act went into effect as an attempt to regulate the sending of unsolicited e-mails, also known as "spam". It was targeted at the spammers who market porn, hot stock tips, pharmaceuticals, and other sundry items which none of us truly want. Alas, this law has changed the face of e-mail marketing.

In a nutshell, the CAN-SPAM Act prohibits unwanted e-mails that trick the recipient into opening the e-mail that they did not give consent for in the first place. Unsolicited e-mails must be clearly identified as advertisements and the recipients need to be able to opt-out of future messages. Unsolicited e-mails must have legitimate e-mail return addresses.

To complicate matters further, over 30 states have adopted anti-spam legislation, with California the most aggressive. The CAN-SPAM Act is intended to override state or local anti-spam laws. Enforcement to date has been modest and is primarily driven by the Federal Trade Commission (FTC). The potential penalties can be significant. Violators are subject to imprisonment for three to five years, fines of $250 per violation (i.e., per e-mail!), and statutory damages that could go as high as $2 Million.

If your company intends to market using unsolicited e-mails, I recommend that you do the following:

- Your firm should author a company policy for unsolicited e-mail. This policy should be posted on the website and placed in the employee manual.
- If possible, use e-mail lists with customers who have consented to receive such mailings.
- Create a client consent form that clearly states to customers what they are going to receive via e-mail; have them fill it out and keep

it on file. This form is typically available at your website. Consent language should be clearly posted on your website

- It should be the company practice to acknowledge and remove opt-out requests promptly; I recommend ten business days or sooner. Same day removal would be best.
- Make sure that any third parties (i.e., channel partners or affiliates) who sell you products play by the same rules as you.
- All e-mails originating from your firm should identify your firm as the sender.
- You must use honest subject lines. Tricking readers to open the e-mail is clever, but is pushing the limit of the law.
- As a rule, don't give your e-mail lists to third parties. This is tricky since affiliates and channel partners often share lists.
- Be sure to include your company's street address and a link to your company's privacy policy in all your e-mail communications.
- Go to http://ftc.gov (the Federal Trade Commission) and familiarize yourself with the act. Do the right thing and obey the law.

More questions? See your attorney.

Action: If you don't have an attorney, ask others that run small businesses for a reference. You might need one someday.

79. *National Do-Not-Call Registry*

"Call me (call me) on the line
Call me, call me any, anytime
Call me (call me) my love
You can call me any day or night
Call me"

Blondie (1980)

If your business markets to consumers using the phone, please read on. By the way, please take me off your call list (just joking).

As of October 1, 2003, it is illegal for telemarketers to call a telephone number listed on the on National-Do-Not Call Registry. Consumers can fight back by registering phone numbers (both landline and cell phone); this registration is good for five years. This restriction applies to any business selling over the phone except for charities, telephone surveys, and political organizations.

If your firm has an existing relationship with the consumer, you are allowed to call them for a period of up to 18 months since the last transaction, but only if they agree to let you call them. If they protest, you have to take them off your list. A consumer who has registered on the list and still receives a telemarketing phone call can file a complaint with the FTC. Violators could be fined up to $11,000 per incident.

You might consider: Contact http://donotcall.gov for more information.

80. Website Visitors Need to Opt-in

"In God we trust, all others we virus scan."

Author Unknown

The best e-mail lists are lists that you created the hard way by capturing addresses one address at a time. When you add a new e-mail address to your list, you are required to inform the visitor about how you are going to use their address. The visitor must give their permission and approve the way in which it will be used. Without this consent, you are a just another spammer.

E-mail addresses have short lives. People change their e-mail addresses with remarkable frequency. NFO Research Group, the large national polling organization, estimates that up to 32% of e-mail addresses are turned over annually. To offset this turnover of your list, be sure to e-mail frequently to catch these changes. This turnover also reinforces the need for using multiple channels of communication with people on your e-mail list. If you send both direct mail and e-mail to your list, you lower the risk of losing touch. The direct mailer can remind people to visit your site; if their e-mail has changed since their last visit, this will give them an opportunity to register again on your site and give you permission again to use their new e-mail address.

Another option for building up your e-mail database would be buying a list. Be sure to find out how the list was developed. There is a technique called doubling, which list makers use to ask the prospect on at least two different occasions for permission to add them to the list. Make sure that the list includes only prospects that have agreed to be on the list. One problem with this approach is the lack of clarity of how this list will be used. When they respond to your e-mail, be sure to ask permission again and clarify how their address will be used.

While it takes time it takes to develop your own list, having your own list is best. There are many ways you can build your e-mail address list.

- Grab business cards from everyone you meet; ask them if you can put them on your list.
- If you do trade shows or conferences with booths, have a drawing for a prize like an iPod or a Blackberry. I used this technique recently for a trade show and received 300 business cards.
- Trade shows often sell the registered attendee lists; this can be a high-value list.

- When customers call your office, ask them for their contact information; hold a contest with your employees to see who can capture the most new e-mail addresses in a day.
- Encourage website visitors to become registered members of your website; suggest to them that they will be able to receive personalized information or alerts via e-mail. Give them a reason or an incentive to register.
- Make e-mail address submission easy to do. If it is a pain to do this, people won't do it.
- Develop a privacy policy and post it on your website. This is a messy subject, since the courts are still sorting this one out. Consult your attorney for the proper language to use.
- E-mail letters with a one click "take me off the list" button are best for you and the recipient of your e-mail. Be sure to respond immediately; auto-response e-mail to the recipient is most effective.

What this means to you: Getting permission to contact your clients by e-mail is not optional; set up an opt-in database immediately. Otherwise, you are a spammer.

81. Don't Worry, Be Happy

"I am an optimist. It does not seem much use being anything else."

Winston Churchill (1874–1965) English statesman

It is hard to be optimistic in our pessimistic world.

Just listen to the evening news report; it seems that nothing good ever happens anymore. News coverage is overwhelmingly pessimistic and negative, since the good things in the world are just boring when compared to a car bombing in the Middle East. Even advertising is negative. Our breath stinks, our hair is dull, and our teeth are yellow. These problems must be fixed, or we will be even more miserable with no friends.

Yet, when we study the aged, we find that they are often optimistic about the future and look back fondly on the past. Studies seem to indicate that a factor in longevity is a sunny attitude or optimism. When successful people are studied, they often exude optimism about the future. They have a strong belief in their personal abilities and know that despite whatever adversity comes their way they will persevere. Positive people tend to focus on the opportunities before them and see possibilities; positive people seem to be able to overlook barriers or constraints.

Yet, pessimism reigns supreme in our society despite the increasing evidence that optimistic people get rewarded with longevity, wealth, success, and happiness. Negative people tend to focus on life's problems, only see limitations, and barriers; negative people tend think of their resources as limited.

Martin Seligman, author of the book LEARNED OPTIMISM, defines the two personality groups as follows:

- Optimists tend to believe that failure is only temporary. It is their perspective that defeat or adversity it not their fault. They feel that these circumstances are just bad luck. They are unfazed by defeat and will react by trying harder to do better.
- Pessimists tend to believe that bad happenings are their fault and that the future is dark and uncertain. They think that the dark days will continue, despite everything they might do to correct it.

Successful entrepreneurs tend to be optimistic and have high levels of job satisfaction. The same applies to successful salespeople; a sunny attitude tends to carry them through the tough times, while the same attitude propels them to even more success. Successful entrepreneurs and sales-people tend to believe what they want to believe, which generally is that the best is yet to come.

My recommendation is to turn off the evening news and watch Seinfeld reruns instead. Read the funny pages and skip the headlines. Hang out with positive people and avoid people with negative attitudes. Take on the behavior of positive people. Use positive expressions, words, and clichés while eliminating negative expressions, words, and clichés. Eliminate "no", "can't", and "but" from your vocabulary; substitute a positive vision with bountiful resources. I have yet to see a barrier so big that I could not walk around it and continue my journey.

Don't worry. Be happy. It pays better.

Self-improvement: Read books that inspire you. As a start, check out FIFTY SELF-HELP CLASSICS: FIFTY INSPIRATIONAL BOOKS TO TRANSFORM YOUR LIFE *by Tom Butler-Bowdon.*

82. All My Friends and Customers Started Out As Strangers

"I get by with a little help from my friends."

John Lennon, The Beatles (1940–1980) Singer, songwriter

All books on marketing need a chapter on the importance of networking and I won't bother reinventing the wheel on this topic. However, here are few rules to go by:

- Always be friendly and always ask others questions about them. Focus the conversation on them; it is all about them and not about you.
- Don't sell. Don't close. The purpose of networking is to connect on a personal level while creating an opportunity for follow up. If you start to sell too soon or close a deal on the spot, you likely will skip a few steps and not get the desired outcome.
- Always follow up. Entering a business card in a contact manager such as Microsoft Outlook or ACT! is a good thing, but you should not stop there. I recommend that you follow up quickly, before your contact forgets meeting you. I would wait no more than two days, at most.
- Always carry plenty of business cards (duh!). Exchange business cards. Offer yours first. If they don't offer theirs, ask them for one. Write notes on the back of their card that include what you promised, the date, and other pertinent information. Consider carrying a digital recorder to capture key information; after you have met someone new and walked away, you can quickly dictate the valuable information learned for retrieval later.
- Don't presume that you understand what others do or what is important to them. Stop yourself from jumping to conclusions. Ask more questions, confirm your understanding. Be an active listener.
- Offer your help. Be interested. Offer a referral. Suggest that you will get back to them. Suggest that you want to learn more.
- Suggest an introduction to someone you know who might prove interesting to them. Offer to meet them for coffee sometime.
- Follow up. Always. Hand-written notes may be best since people

will read them. Suggest a meeting, deliver the reference, etc. If you follow up with a note card, include a comment about something they said, preferably something personal about them. Try to connect as a friend. E-mail is instantaneous, but pedestrian. Leaving voice mails works too, but don't expect a call back.

- How often can you call them? This is tricky. How often would you want to be contacted? A note card with a phone call would be OK to me. A follow-up call about a week later is fine. After that, you may appear to be a stalker or an insurance salesman. In selling, calling up to five times with messages left behind is a good number. When networking, I find it to be more delicate. A final follow-up message suggesting that was nice to meet them, while letting them know it is fine for them to call you back may be the final step.

- Sometimes people don't call back. People are busy and it may be a matter of timing. It can be the method of communication; I have had people not return my phone calls but when I e-mailed them, I got an immediate response. So, try a different method if you are not successful in connecting on the first try.

- People also need a reason or incentive to call you back. What value is there for them to call you back? While some people may call you back with little or no incentive, most won't. My personal rule is to always call back once, even if it is a call from an insurance salesman. However, I may be different from most people.

- I recommend that you read the book NEVER EAT ALONE: AND OTHER SECRETS TO SUCCESS, ONE RELATIONSHIP AT A TIME by Keith Ferrazzi. His message is simple and you can put it to action immediately. He emphasizes the importance of having access to people of power and influence. He reminds you to not keep score on who last corresponded to whom; rather, he encourages you to give unconditionally since you will be rewarded later. He also suggests that you network all the time and not just when you need it.

- Finally, treat everyone you meet as if they were a VIP. Someday they may be. Be kind to the little people. Don't make enemies and don't burn bridges. They may be needed tomorrow. Stay in touch always.

Late night reading: PERMISSION MARKETING: TURNING STRANGERS INTO FRIENDS AND FRIENDS INTO CUSTOMERS by Seth Godin

83. The Truth, the Whole Truth, and Nothing But the Truth

"If you tell the truth you don't have to remember anything."

Mark Twain (1835–1910) Humorist, author and wit

Tell people the truth and you will get what you want. Exaggerate, lie, fib, or try to be something that you are not and people will see right through you and they will pass on what you are trying to sell them.

When you are wrong, admit it. Humans are tolerant and an honest man is very appreciated in our society. An example is a recall of a product problem by General Motors; when a recall announcement is made and the public learns of the defect, the consumer forgives GM for the error. What is left in the public's mind is the image of GM trying to make things safer or better.

Unfortunately, the political spin masters and the big PR machines often head the other direction, which is ill advised in my opinion. Bill Clinton, when confronted about his indiscretions with Monica Lewinsky, repeatedly denied the claims (under oath as I recall). Later, he recanted his story and apologized. The best course of action would have been to tell the truth at the beginning and move on. Despite his lies, the nation did forgive him, more or less.

Honesty is valued highly by the customer, but the customer has learned not to trust nor believe what they are told. This particularly applies to salespeople and I believe that this distrust is warranted. Too many years of interfacing with manipulative sales reps who tell the truth only when it is expedient have soured the purchasing community.

The lesson for a business is to market your product enthusiastically, but accurately. Never take on an assignment or a commitment that you really cannot do well. This means committing to do only what is truly possible, to always tell the truth even when it means admitting a mistake or weakness, and to always follow up on your commitments. Some ideas for marketing with more integrity:

- Avoid selling by telling; instead, listen first and strive to be more collaborative. "Old school" selling encouraged the stereotype of a fast-talking sales rep that wouldn't let the customer speak. Try the reverse; see how little you need to say by listening more actively.

- Don't commit too soon. Agreeing to do the work or ship the product before you truly understand the opportunity can be a serious misstep. Slow down to understand the customer requirements more exactly. Then, if your solution fits, you can commit.
- An old saying that still reverberates with authenticity is to "under commit and over deliver". Exceeding customer expectations is a great way to sell with integrity.
- Offering a satisfaction guarantee helps eliminate the fear of making a wrong decision by the client. Watch the customer sigh with relief when the penalty for buying the wrong thing is eliminated.
- Don't force your agenda on the client. This gets back to understanding the customer's needs and not offering your solution too early.
- References are more believable than anything that you can say. Always have positive references available to help the customer understand your capabilities.
- Say "no" to things you cannot do. This may be hard because so many entrepreneurs have such a strong belief in themselves and their firm's abilities to stretch and make the impossible happen. If you can't do a great job or if your product is not a great fit, just say no. You will get another chance.
- Testimonials can quiet the strongest objections. Video testimonials on your website can be very powerful. The same applies to written testimonials in your marketing materials.
- Show your customers evidence of your success, quality, and capabilities. This could be a testimonial, or this might be showing your in-house records for quality, accuracy, or on-time delivery. The latter is a dramatic gesture that lays it all out for the customers to see; symbolically it says that you have nothing to hide.

One more comment: Review your brochure materials; do they accurately state your capabilities? Are your specifications up-to-date?

84. *Your Own Personal Board of Directors*

"When the student is ready, the master appears."

Buddhist Proverb

Often entrepreneurs find themselves needing advice and counsel; worse, they are just plain lonely. This vacuum can be very prevalent at small businesses and, by definition, exists for the "solopreneurs" (the individual business person).

Frankly, few of us really are multi-talented and this can quickly be brought into focus when you start a company or go off on your own in a small business. Running your own business requires you to be an accountant, marketing guru, an operations manager, and a human resources manager, to name a few of the skills required.

You really have no choice but to look outside and ask for help. You can pay for this counsel or you can get it free; either way most of us need it. I recommend that you set up your own personal board of directors. Look for people who know what you don't. This could include law, managing people, sales and marketing, finance, spirituality, real estate, technology, and others. They must be willing to help you. You probably have friends who support you already. What I suggest is that you take the next step and formalize the relationship.

First, you need to identify the people who have the knowledge, expertise, and contacts that you don't. They could be friends, relatives, neighbors, colleagues, and strangers. Just about all my friends started out as strangers, so don't let the fact that you don't know someone stop you. You are looking for people who also have the desire to coach, teach, or share.

Next, meet with them in a casual setting one on one; I like a business lunch best, but that is up to you. At this meeting, a key objective is to explain your admiration for their skills and how you don't have the same skills. This disclosure can be powerful for you and for them. Most people need to be needed and will bend over backwards to help you. Ninety-nine times out of one hundred, your prospective personal board of director will be complimented by the words and they will admire your self-disclosure. Most will agree to help you on the spot. It is just that easy.

From there, it is up to you, but I recommend that you make a point of meeting, phoning, or e-mailing your individual board members monthly.

Keep them updated on your progress, successes, and failures. Be gracious and thankful. Look for ways to give back and help them. The goal is to set up a friendship or bond similar to that of a coach and player. The coach gives and the players gets. My personal experience as a coach is that I have been paid back in full many times over. You will find this same attitude with most people who are willing to join your board.

Your do list: Write down a list of the type of support you will need from your own personal board of directors? Who do you admire that you can invite to join your board?

85. Focus and It Will Expand

"While we are focusing on fear, worry, or hate, it is not possible for us to be experiencing happiness, enthusiasm or love."

Bo Bennett (1972–) Businessman

I am not a psychotherapist and I don't pretend to be one. However, I do know that if you can visualize a goal and commit to making it happen, it can be achieved.

Let's say you want to be the best at something or, at least, really good. For this example, let's focus on getting better at golf. Of course, if you want to be a better golfer you will need the basic equipment, you will need instruction, and you will need to golf a lot. Conveniently, golf has a game score, which allows you to measure your progress. If your golf game is in the low 90s and you want to improve, pick a challenging goal like shooting in the low 80s, which is excellent for an amateur golfer.

The next step is to personally commit to the goal. Write it down. Tell people about it. Go to bed at night thinking about averaging in the low 80s. Carry the written goal in your wallet or purse. Pull it out and look at it through out your day. Be the goal, so to speak. With the goal to guide you, do all the little things right and often. Clean your equipment and play an additional 18 holes when time allows. Read biographies of great golfers. Watch the Golf Channel. Hang out at the club. Talk about golf.

Seek advice and instruction. Find a coach or instructor to help you perfect your game. Be open to feedback and make changes. Olympic athletes win gold medals on the practice field first by making each practice count. It is not luck that gets the gold medal; it is hard work and dedication that makes the difference. Sure, physical ability helps, but attitude and commitment are the true enablers of success.

Focus and it will expand. The more you think about something, the bigger and more powerful it becomes whether that thought is positive or negative. Have you ever noticed that when you when you decide to buy a new car, maybe like a Corvette, everybody else seems to have one? Every time you drive down the highway, there are Corvettes everywhere. This is no accident. By focusing on the Corvette, your awareness of Corvettes becomes greater.

The same focus can mistakenly be targeted at negative thoughts and goals. Do you ever get up in the morning and think negative thoughts like, "I don't want to work today" or "Why do I need to go to school?" These negative thoughts can enable failure if you let them. Replace those negative thoughts with positive messages. Read positive literature. Post positive quotes on the mirror in the bathroom. If you catch yourself being negative, try to stop yourself immediately and switch to words that are more positive.

You can achieve goals by focusing on them. Thinking about your goals is powerful, but you need to put them in writing to give them life; this could start with your mission statement and progress to your business plan. Commit yourself to these goals by publicly announcing them to family, friends and colleagues; have them help you achieve these goals by involving them.

Late night reading: LEARNED OPTIMISM: HOW TO CHANGE YOUR MIND AND YOUR LIFE by Martin Seligman

86. *Opportunity Won't Wait For You*

"Luck is what happens when preparation meets opportunity."

Seneca (54 B.C.-39 A.D.) Roman philosopher

Living and working in the new millennium requires that you always be ready. In sports, the coach tells you to stay on the balls of your feet, which is the "ready stance". This is especially true in football where by staying ready you can avoid injury; the expression being caught flat-footed means you got knocked to the ground since you were unprepared.

Sure, you are smart, professional, and damned good lookin', but the question is are you ready if an opportunity presented itself right now? Make it so. Prepare yourself for the unexpected by letting others know that you are ready and available if needed; stay current on technology, read the business best sellers (like FIRST, BEST, or DIFFERENT), keep your resume up-to-date and be a continuous learner. Opportunities come with little warning and will pass by quickly.

Opportunities can appear out of nowhere and you need to be prepared to react. To be ready, stay out of debt: don't buy expensive houses or fancy cars. Massive debt may motivate some, but for most of us, debt functions as a ball and chain keeping us from taking risks. Often opportunity knocks, but requires relocation with great speed. Having too many expensive toys will slow you down and will keep you from taking a chance on something new.

Be mobile. Be fluid. Be ready. Don't be judgmental. Shut up and listen. Observe. Seldom is the idea for a new product or business a supernova knocking at your door. More likely, it starts as a ray of light or a thought that just won't go away. Keep a note pad or recorder by your bedside for the idea that floats through your mind as you try to go to sleep.

For a business, marketing opportunities may present themselves in different forms such as a competitor that fails to deliver on time, a customer who describes a new problem that has been keeping him or her up at night, or it could be a new piece of equipment that will make you more efficient back at the shop.

An entrepreneur stays ready for opportunity by:

- Carefully managing your debt; living below your means.
- Paying your bills on time.
- Having adequate credit lines for new ventures, it is much easier to get credit when you don't need it.

- Being adequately insured in case of fire, flood, and earthquake.
- Carrying "key man insurance" for the irreplaceable executives (that means you).
- Having documented customer and/or personal references, these are hard to get on short notice.
- Having an up-to-date business plan; you should do a full review annually and monitor this quarterly.
- Building strong supplier relationships. Suppliers want to know that they are valued and not just when you need help.
- Treating employees as trusted partners; valued employees will leap over tall buildings when you need him to.
- Planning for succession in the business. Who will run the ship if you are ill or go on disability?
- Giving back to the community through charity work, volunteering, and board membership. Opportunity is most often relationship driven, so be out there in the community or the industry.

Conversely, if a business doesn't ready itself by doing the above, marketing opportunities will pass it by.

Action: Update your resume or biography.

87. Procrastination is a Business Killer

"A good plan, violently executed now, is better than a perfect plan next week."

George Patton (1885–1945) U.S. General

In the new millennium, speed is sometimes more important than substance. The pace of work has radically changed over the last decade largely due to the internet. Gone are the days of mailing the proposal to a customer; instead they want it now (i.e., today and not later) and if you cannot deliver it now, they can find others that will.

This faster pace requires the entrepreneur to be focused on what is important. This starts with the mission and the values of the business, which act as a compass. After that, you are left with the difficult task of priority setting while you constantly adjust to the changing needs of your target market. There seems so little time as the phone rings, the e-mails ping away, and the voice mail fills. Maybe you can wait until later. I think not.

Procrastination is a killer of businesses. Maybe better described as fear, procrastination just does not make good business sense. If you procrastinate, someone else will beat you. It is just that simple. Often decisions are hard to make because we are afraid to make them and because we are unaccustomed to making them quickly.

Practically speaking, this means that all phone messages need to be returned today and not tomorrow. If you have an 800 line, make sure that it is closely monitored and that the appropriate action (returned call or otherwise) is taken. The same applies to e-mails from customers; in the era of the Blackberry, many people want instant results and that means an instant reply from you. To get around this time pressure, a quick acknowledgment can buy you additional time, but be sure to follow up as promised. Promises must be delivered on time with no exceptions. Make it a rule to promise a lot and deliver more. Deliver it early if you can.

A technique that helps beat procrastination and is easy to implement, is giving an unpleasant task fifteen minutes of your time. Schedule yourself for only fifteen minutes to tackle the task, give it your best, and then stop. Guess what? You just got started. Conversely, you can reward yourself with fifteen-minute breaks. After tackling a difficult task, give yourself a fifteen-minute break for a walk, a nap, or listen to your favorite music.

Another use of the fifteen-minute break is to schedule your tasks for one hour, but conclude your work in forty-five minutes so you can take a fifteen-minute break to refresh yourself.

Some other techniques to beat procrastination include:

- Make a public decree that you will get the job done. Simply, tell others that you will get this job done today. Commit to the task now and give others the responsibility to nag you.
- Do the hard stuff first. Tackle the tough task first; it will amaze you how good it makes you feel. This will empower you to get the rest of your work done.
- Keep score on the important activities that you tend to procrastinate. It may be returned calls, adding names to your e-mail list, or writing handwritten note cards. Schedule time to do these dirty jobs and get them done.

Put down the book and do this right now: What is the biggest problem that keeps you up at night? Take the next fifteen minutes and create an action plan to solve it. Ready, set, go.

88. A Few Words on Business Cards

"Tell me and I'll forget. Show me and I'll remember. Involve me and I'll understand."

Confucius (551–479 B.C.) Chinese philosopher

The ubiquitous business card is a critical tool for communicating your brand. Make sure it reflects your image and that you maximize its usefulness. Here are a few do's and don'ts regarding business cards:

- Print the card using color. Study after study shows that color printing significantly impacts the readers' ability to notice and remember.
- Don't cram too much printing or too many images on the card; leave white space for an easy-to-read look.
- If you have your photo on your card, have a professional photographer take your photo; look your best. The photo card is a common practice in some industries such as real estate.
- Include your tagline and logo. Beware that some logos look great when full-sized but lose detail when shrunk down for a business card. This is a design issue to avoid. In addition, some businesses or industries don't put logos on cards; beware of protocol.
- Make sure that the information on the card is typo free and accurate. If the information changes, buy new cards. Handwritten corrections look amateurish.
- Use a standard-size card, since business card storage systems presume a standard size and shape.
- Get your cards printed professionally on quality paper; although the do-it-yourself business cards for the laser printer are getting better, they still look homemade to me.
- Include all pertinent information such phone, fax, website, e-mail address, mail address, cell phone, etc. Duh!
- The back of the card is a great place for a mission statement, product information, or something that you want to communicate to everyone.
- Don't put pricing on the back since business cards are evergreen and prices are not.
- It is OK to list services or products on the card, but remember that plans change and your cards could quickly be obsolete if you make changes to your product line.

- Your business cards should reflect the theme, color, and logo used in all your marketing communications including your website. Send a consistent message.

For the "to do" list: If the back of your business card is blank, put it to work by adding your mission statement.

89. Note Card Follow-Up

"Don't miss the donut by looking through the hole."

Author Unknown

The internet age is one that has lost its personal touch, if not its humanity. Little personalization is done. Everything is digitized, automated, and delivered but is done without compassion or style. Letters are addressed to "Dear Occupant"; "Please insert your name here." Seemingly, every letter received has a label created from a database by printer. Often misspelled and with wrong annotations, they are dispassionate and rude. Therefore, we toss them in the trash without opening them. Worse, yet, e-mails bombard us daily to such an extent that we filter them for spam such as mail from strangers, salespeople, and lost relatives; even with this editing, we still pound away at the delete key. Who wants all this junk mail?

Note cards are mail that always gets opened. The "retro power" of the handwritten note card is now truly amazing. When an envelope comes to your name and address written in cursive, don't you open it first? This is the appeal of the handwritten note card, arguably a relic from the past, but an effective tool in our sterile internet age.

I recommend that you go to the local printer and get stationery made on good paper with professionally printed letterhead. Note cards give a personal touch in our depersonalized world. Always handwrite the address on the envelope. Don't use labels or printed envelopes and always use a real stamp. Make it look like a party invitation or, better yet, a love letter.

Say thanks. Congratulate. Don't qualify or demean these acts of kindness and generosity with limiting words or thoughts. If you like someone or something, say it. For example, if you want to congratulate someone on a job well done, write that. Then back it up with evidence. Cite an example. Avoid using qualifying or demeaning words like "This is just a note to say thanks." What do you mean "just a note?" Instead, say thanks and give a reason why.

Give compliments and avoid flattery. When you compliment someone or something, explain why and give an example. A compliment without evidence is just flattery. Flattery is not remembered and is not as believable. Compliments are remembered, if not cherished. Say it with a handwritten note card today.

Action Item: Go to the printer and order personalized note cards with envelopes that match your business card (i.e. paper, color, ink, typeface, etc)

90. *Direct Marketing with Postcards*

"I have received no more than one or two letters in my life that were worth the postage."

Henry David Thoreau (1817–1862)
American essayist, poet, and philosopher

While the internet has opened up an incredible new channel to communicate with customers and prospects, postcards remain a very effective way to communicate with your target market. Unlike an e-mail, which can be deleted without being opened, postcards get read right away.

I recommend using standard-sized post cards (4.125" x 6") since they are cheap; mail costs are about 40% the cost of a letter, yet they get delivered as first-class mail. Some will argue for odd-sized or unusually-shaped cards so that they stick out of the mail pile; they cost more and I don't believe that they get read more than other cards, although they might get read first or sooner. I also suggest using real stamps instead of imprinted postage; it looks friendlier and seems less like a direct-mail campaign.

The outstanding benefit of postcards is that your message gets delivered and read with high frequency; people have to read it before they throw it away. If the card is undeliverable, it gets returned to you and this allows you to improve your customer database. Since it is a very personal form of communication, your competitors won't find out about it.

Postcard direct mailers need to be simple. If the purpose of the postcard is to create a lead, deliver one message only. Be sure to give the reader instructions on what to do next: go to website or call or write. If you are promoting an event, give just the details about the event and no more. I suggest leaving white space on the card in effort to make it friendly for the reader. Don't cram it with details since it likely won't get read. If you are trying to create brand awareness, you can use four-color printing. This will keep the consistency of your brand.

Given the choice between sending one wave of direct mailers to many or multiple direct mailers to a smaller audience, go for the latter. Relationships are built by multiple contacts and there is no substitute in marketing for frequency of contact. The marketing term for a successful contact is called "reach"; it is marketing legend that a contact or reach without frequency makes for wasted money. One wave of direct mail just won't do much. Generally, three waves is a minimum in a direct mail campaign with the wave's spaced every two weeks or so. Some experts will argue for more waves, but the advent of spam has made people less tolerant.

Something to do: Review your incoming mail carefully for direct mail postcards. Look for clever ideas, colors that grab you, and calls to action. Save the ones that you like.

91. Show and Sell With Video

"The movies are the only business where you can go out front
and applaud yourself."

Will Rogers (1879–1935) Actor, cowboy, and wit

Video technology is getting cheaper and friendlier; small businesses can now produce their own videos to help market their products. Videos can be great selling tools in lieu of a traditional brochure, which can be direct-mailed, handed out a trade show, or archived on your website.

Here are a few of the basics about video marketing:

- Great videos start with a great script, which is the roadmap for getting your marketing message properly documented. Determine the message you want to deliver; remember that people will remember only two or three basic points from a speech or from a video. Divide the script into three parts: first, focus on the needs or problems of the customer; second, focus on the benefits of your solution; and three, create a call for action.
- Your video should last no more than five minutes, so you have to keep the message very simple.
- Insert a customer testimonial in the video; happy customers are your best salespeople. Interview a customer on video and add their comments; tie their comments to your benefits.
- Avoid video special effects since they distract the viewer and give the video a "slick or produced feel"; it is a better to deliver a message that is personal and unpretentious.
- Video producers are available for outsourcing this type of work; if this video will be viewed by thousands of customers and the content will have a long life, it could be money well spent to have a professional help you. Beware that the costs can be significant. If this video will viewed by dozens instead of thousands and the content is subject to change, you can do it yourself.
- A small business should not use professional actors, but a professional voice or narrator can add clarity to the presentation.
- Close-up photography works best. Use a tripod to stabilize the image. Still photographs can be inserted, but remember that they can be seen on the screen for only a few seconds. Music is a nice touch for background effects. The software to produce this type of video is surprisingly inexpensive.

- Test your video with friends and clients. Edit non-essential content out. Once released, track your leads and sales results that comes because this medium.

After work tonight: Pull out the video camera and let someone record you talking about your business. Talk about what you know about the customers and their special needs. This could be the first take on your video.

92. Direct Marketing Helps You Build Relationships

"There comes a time in every man's life and I've had many of them."

Casey Stengel (1890–1975) Baseball manager

Here are a few direct marketing ideas that have worked for me:

- One direct marketing idea I have found that really works is to handwrite addresses on envelopes with beautiful handwriting. OK, if you are like me, you will need to find someone to do that. Now this may sound a bit sexist, but if you are marketing to a predominantly male audience, have someone with a pretty or feminine cursive style address the envelopes. They will get opened. Use real stamps and add a drop of perfume to the envelope as a special, fragrant ingredient. Sounds corny? It works.
- Another trick is the "faux referral". I have seen this done with remarkable results. Cut out a magazine or newspaper advertisement for your product or service and add a yellow post-it note. Handwrite on the post-it something like "Try this is. It really works". Sign it as JJ or some other initial/s or first name. Direct mail it to key executives or decision makers at your prospective customers. The recipient gets the ad with the post-it and asks the question who is JJ? Next, they read the advertisement and if your advertisement is written correctly, it includes your contact information and a call for action such as a discount. Try this. It really works. JJ
- I also like the faux wedding invitation. This is a fun way to market an event with a modest distribution list. Go to the local printer and get embossed wedding invitations. Handwrite the addresses as before. Include an RSVP card. People always open wedding invitations. This is a great way to market an event. It does not have to be an event at all. It could be a promotion that includes a coupon. Remember that your objective is to get the envelope opened and read. What you put inside is your business.
- I have a friend named Jim Kelton who runs a small IT services firm in Irvine, California, called Altius Information Technologies. For years, Jim struggled to market his services to small- and

medium-sized enterprises. He spent big bucks advertising and had nothing to show for his money. Direct mailers didn't work either. All he got in return for his hard work was silence. One day he sent out a small mailing to a list of prospects (maybe fifty or so); the mailing included a letter describing his services and a one-dollar bill. Guess what? The phone rang. He did it again, but this time he sent the letter out with a two-dollar bill. The phone rang again. No three-dollar bill you say? Jim had one printed. When Jim followed up on the phone with the people on his mailing list, he referred to himself as the "money man"; everyone knew who he was. One prospect told him that he was waiting for the five-dollar bill. Although it would be hard to scale Jim's direct mail campaign with hard cash, it shows that being different matters when you do direct mail.

- If you are in a service business, consider offering a 30-day free trial. If your service delivers value, they might just commit for an extended period. Be careful with this technique; it important to make sure the trial directly involves the decision maker and to make sure that the prospect is well qualified. Life is short. You don't need to waste your valuable time and resources on someone that is not a qualified decision maker.

- When using a promotional letter instead of a brochure, be sure to use a P.S. (i.e., a postscript). A postscript is highly likely to be read. Write the postscript as if it were written to a friend; include one final benefit with a request for action. (Like "Call my 800 number.")

- A guarantee of satisfaction is a compelling benefit in a direct mailer. Guarantees can push aside objections. See the chapter on guarantees.

- Consider the use of a testimonial in your promotional letter. Prospects find testimonials far more powerful than a list of benefits from you. Tie the testimonial to the benefit by placing it in close proximity to the benefit it references on the mailer.

- Consider three-dimensional or box mailers instead of flat envelopes. Studies have shown that boxes get opened at a 99% rate, while flat mailers can just end up in the trash, unopened. Here is an example of a 3-D mailer that had a tremendous open and response rate. A software provider mailed a small box that contained a letter, a software demonstration on a compact disc, and some loose peanuts. On the outside of the box was the phrase, "What you need are good people, not a bunch of nuts." A clever phrase got the recipient's attention, but the rattling of the peanuts proved most compelling. The response rate was off the charts.

- Can't get a key prospect to call you back? Consider sending a cell phone with 100 free (i.e. prepaid) minutes. Include a note that says, "Enjoy the phone and please call me." I tried this crazy technique when I was a sales manager in the financial services business. My sales team came up with a short list of 30 CFOs (Chief Financial Officers), who would not return our calls. We sent the phones with the letter. Over half of the CFOs called us and we got appointments set up with many of them. Some of them just sent the phone back, while a few used the phones and did not call us. From my sales team's perspective, the campaign was a huge success.

Tip: Test the three-dimensional mailer with a small group of prospects; be sure to give them a call to action with an incentive. If it works, try a larger mailing.

93. Be a Knowledge Broker

"Knowledge is power."

Sir Francis Bacon (1561–1626) Philosopher

Be an expert in your field. One of the best ways to get your message out is to soft sell it through a promotion technique that I call being a "knowledge broker". This means speaking authoritatively on subjects germane to your business at trade shows, industry events, and conferences while getting published via quotes in the local newspaper and industry trade journals. Create an image for yourself by being a quoted expert in your field of expertise.

Your objective as a knowledge broker is to establish yourself as knowledgeable and trustworthy; you are not directly selling your products or services. Your goal is to educate the reader or listener while building your personal brand. The last thing your audience wants is a sales pitch. Instead, tell compelling stories which people will remember and retell themselves. Facts and figures are seldom remembered.

When preparing your message as a knowledge broker, focus on the wants or needs of your customer, rather than on your product or solution. Identify the problems that a customer is trying to solve and the questions that they want answered. Help them answer these questions. Brand your message with a clever title to help people remember it. (This is marketing after all.)

To make this a lead-generation tool, have a printed copy of your speech or a summary of your main points available as a handout with your contact information. A DVD or CD might be better; you can repurpose these tools on your website as white papers or articles. You can also use this summary in your day-to-day selling; offer the document to customers and prospects when on the phone or when meeting in person. It can take the form of a gift.

At the event, be sure to carry plenty of business cards, hang around the event, and meet people. Stay in the moment. Often I will see speakers rush off the stage to catch a cab to airport. Don't waste the opportunity to make new friends and create leads.

You should try this: Write a letter to the editor of the local newspaper or industry publication about an issue or event that is pertinent to your business. You will be amazed at how often these letters get published.

94. How to Give a Speech that Sells

"Quote me as saying I was misquoted."

Groucho Marx (1890–1977) Comedian and author

Public speaking is one of best ways to create publicity for you and business, while positioning yourself as a knowledge broker. Speaking at an industry gathering such as a trade show or a conference gives you a forum to be an expert. Speaking at such an event helps your target market recognize the unique knowledge that you possess about their needs and their problems.

When choosing your topic for your speech, you need to figure out what problems or issues your customers are struggling with today; you should focus on a topic that has great importance or urgency to them. Of course, the topic needs to be one of which you have considerable expertise in while also fitting your firm's product or solution. While not a sales pitch for your product, the goal is to demonstrate your firm's awareness of the problem and your understanding of how it impacts the customer. One way to choose the topic is to ask your current customers what is bugging them most today or what keeps them up late at night. Let their pain help you choose your topic.

As far as where to speak or at what event, I recommend that you choose events that are frequently attended by your customers. Once again, your customers can tell you what events they attend and which events provide the most value. Likely, you will find there are many events to choose from, yet few that your customers find valuable. Often these events have a focus or an agenda that is too broad for them or is largely not relevant. Your participation at such an event might make it more relevant to them.

Conferences and trade shows may provide the event or platform for the publicity that can define you as a knowledge broker. Surprisingly, these events often struggle to find good speakers and always need backup speakers. Most of these events are held annually with planning beginning a year in advance. Often the keynote speaker, who may charge huge speaking fees, is the big decision for the conference planners and the big draw for attendees. Yet, these events are often structured with many speakers, panel discussions, and break out rooms. Speakers are needed for all of them.

Having been in the conference business, I can tell you it is very difficult to find quality speakers. It is rare to find a speaker with a solid understanding of the audience's pain who can also deliver an informative and entertaining talk. Those speakers who can deliver that combination of relevant topic and entertainment are in high demand on the speaker circuit. Why not you?

Knowing that the events are planned well in advance, contact the conference organization to identify who is on next year's conference-planning committee. My experience is that the people on the planning committee are often folks just like you who have the same motivation to create a name for themselves. Simple as it sounds, all you need to do is call them up and arrange a lunch to discuss your interest in the event and describe your knowledge of the audience's issues. You could even volunteer to help organize the event, since most of these organizations are staffed with volunteers. You may not be a big-name keynote speaker, but your insider's view could make you a compelling speaker candidate and get you on the agenda. You could get positioned as a backup candidate. The good news is that speakers cancel with great frequency at the last minute, leaving the conference planners with holes in the agenda and potentially embarrassing situations.

The best-case scenario is to be a named a speaker on the agenda with a topic that is tailored for the audience. Typical conferences and trade shows will promote the event many weeks in advance on their website, in newspapers or trade journals, and using other media. The potential exposure can be incredible. I worked with a technology conference event in Los Angeles that had a professed goal to "blanket the earth" with their conference brochures which were direct-mailed to the mail list; this list included 75,000 names of executives. Additionally, they advertised in the LOS ANGELES TIMES and e-mailed their previous attendees. In the advertising game, that means hundreds of thousands of "impressions", where your name gets displayed as an industry expert or knowledge broker. Trust me, you could not afford to buy this type of advertising, and you can get it by picking up the phone and asking to help.

If you are going to be a presenter at an upcoming trade show or event, be sure to post this event on your website. This could be a topic for a press release. If you have a newsletter, include the topic and event details.

You will need to develop a biography for yourself that touts your credentials. The "bio" should summarize your achievements pertinent to this event including job history, papers published, speeches made, boards that you have served on, etc. Include a quote from the press or another industry expert about you or your company. This is a time to brag, so find a good quote that describes how significant you are. If you don't have one, ask a prominent friend to author one for you. This adds extra punch to an otherwise dry biography. Also, get a professionally done photograph for posting in the brochure or on the website. Often, the conference will require a black and white photo; sometimes color is requested. Have both photos taken since this will be a good investment that you can use again.

As for the speech itself, remember that your audience will likely only remember two or three key points regardless of how long you speak. With so much stimulation and information at trade shows or conferences, the audience can be numb or desensitized and just can't retain much content. So, keep your message simple.

Always start you speech by describing your speech's purpose and main point. Don't dally or filibuster. Get right to the point. In this case, describe what you understand to be the audience's pain. Give examples and tell stories. As mentioned previously, facts tell while stories sell. Give a real-life example of how a firm or individual faced the same pain. Speak in plain terms as if you were speaking to a friend or family member. Don't use overly formal language or phrases. Talk their language. Be yourself.

Next, talk about possible solutions, both good and bad. Give examples. Summarize the solutions and show which works best. Tell another story about how someone used this solution effectively. Close the speech by restating the pain while offering the best solution to remedy the pain. Whether your speech is five minutes or an hour, this same basic structure applies.

Rehearse the speech until you can know it cold; never ever read your speech. I worked with a speech consultant a few years ago who was hired to help my company deliver a road show pitch. Her goal was to help us make the best road show pitch possible. I was stunned to hear her say that to really internalize a speech (to become one with speech) you need to practice the speech start to finish 16 times! She suggested that the average public speaker seldom practiced a speech more than a couple of times, which is the root cause of lousy, meandering speeches.

Stay in tune with your audience. Watch their body language. If you see them nodding off, ask for feedback or questions. Get them involved. Keep them interested. Use vocal variety and be animated. Jokes are fine, but don't overdo it; be aware that the use of ethnic humor, sexual innuendo, and profanity is certain to backfire. Use industry jargon only if you know it and only if the audience will understand it; otherwise, it might sound like you are speaking a foreign language. If you are running long on your speech, go to the conclusion and summarize. Never go long since you might get the hook from the moderator, which could be very embarrassing and will be remembered.

When closing the speech, give the audience a reason and a way to contact you. For example, you could offer a white paper that you have written on this topic; send them to your website to get a copy. I like to use a "landing page" on my website which offers them other material on the topic. You can also suggest that the audience catch you at the break for a copy of the speech or white paper. If you have a blog, let them know about it and how to find it. Remember to bring plenty of business cards to hand out to the people who want to meet you and thank you for a great speech. Be sure to get theirs in return. Another trick is to offer a chance to win a sample of your product or solution or maybe a gift by having the audience members drop a business card in a fishbowl at the back of the room. It may sound hokey, but people like freebies.

Most important is to follow up with every person who gives you a card or who contacts you or hits your website. Ask them what they thought of the speech and ask them about their pain. Send them thank you notes. Add them to your customer database. Let the selling begin. Presuming you do a good job as a speaker and that you stay in touch with the conference planning committee, you will likely be invited back.

To become a better speaker, I highly recommend that you join Toastmasters International, a worldwide non-profit volunteer based public speaking club. Toastmasters International has hundreds of thousands of members with clubs everywhere. I benefited immensely from this organization and I recommend it to anyone who wants to be a better speaker. Go to www.toastmasters.org

A fun thing to try: Go audit a local Toastmasters club and see what it is like.

95. Negotiating for Fun and Profit

"Those are my principles, and if you don't like them…
well, I have others."

Groucho Marx (1890–1977) Comedian and author

Some believe that negotiation is only about thinking quickly on your feet and standing firm. I disagree. Negotiating is hard work and requires intense preparation. I have found that the best negotiators invest significant time doing the following:

- Define an objective. What do you want? What do you need?
- Creating or maintaining the relationship should be the basis of the negotiation, with collaboration as the goal. Speak openly about each other's interests and motivations.
- Understand what the other side wants and needs. A big mistake made by negotiators is not taking the time to listen to what the other side hopes to achieve.
- Don't take an all or nothing position. This creates a win/lose scenario, which often ends in no deal at all. Rather, seek an outcome that allows both parties to get what they need. This provides a platform to do business again.
- Listen more than you speak. If there is ever a time to be an active listener, it is when you negotiate. When in doubt, say nothing.
- Be flexible. Through good listening, you can learn new ways to improve the deal.
- Don't offer your bottom line too early. While it is true that you will need to say what you want to ensure that you get it (at least most of the time), don't speak to too early. It is often said that he who speaks first in a negotiation loses; while this is may be true sometimes, let's just say you don't want to weigh anchor too early. Rather, continue your focus on understanding the needs of the other party.
- Be open and be creative. You might learn something new or get more than you wanted. Be flexible.
- Be fair. A good deal is one that both parties feel good about. If both parties get to win, you will likely have the chance to do business again.

- Sell and negotiate simultaneously. Emphasize benefits of your product as you negotiate. Show the buyer why they need you. Weave this through the steps of the negotiation.
- Commitment is the end game. Getting an agreement in writing with both parties is a must. Verbal contracts only set you up for problems in the future. Some people have such strong egos that they can rationalize any behavior, including reneging on deals. Written contracts are needed for when things don't go right or when someone breaks a promise.
- Don't give up; keep trying. This is hard work. It is desirable to cut a deal in a single session, but this is not always the case. If things seem irresolvable, agree to table the meeting and to come back the next day. Perseverance and preparation pay off. If things are at a total impasse, it may mean one of the parties has goals that are not realistic. Maybe things need to be rethought by both parties.
- Make the pie bigger. Instead of reducing your offer by discounting, consider adding other things to the deal. Give a win to other party by adding new benefits while defending your original proposal. For example, let's say that you offer a PC with accounting software at a sales price of $1,500. Your customer demands a discount of 10%. Instead of discounting the price, include some software that has a list price of $150 (and an actual cost of $50). Although a modest compromise, it might be enough to close the deal.
- Offer multiple, but equal alternatives. Often salespeople offer multiple proposals with one being high, one being medium, and one being bare bones. Often the high offer is heavily discounted, the medium deal is the anticipated deal, and the bare bones deal is the least attractive alternative. Try offering the desired deal, but in three configurations with the same price or near equivalent price. The other party may find one of the configurations much more attractive than the other two and may eagerly agree to a deal allowing both parties to win.

Practice Time: Next time that you are making a significant purchase, ask the sales rep to improve the price. Say something like, "I hadn't intended to buy today, but if you can move on the price a bit, I could buy today". Don't be confrontational, but be assertive. Watch what happens and learn from it. You may get a lower price.

96. *Increasing Profits by Playing it Smart*

"It's not that I'm so smart, it's just that I stay with problems longer."

Albert Einstein (1879–1955) Scientist and mathematician

It is tough out there. Defending your pricing can be hard because of shrewd negotiators, dumb competitors, and careless marketers. Margin is tough to maintain with the daily grind of increasing supplier costs and inflationary pressures. Yet, vigilant entrepreneurs can increase profits every day by slowing down to make profit a daily priority. Simple as it sounds, profit needs to be a daily entry in your Day Timer or on your Palm Pilot.

Make it a daily practice to measure everything that you can. Measure your margin by product, by sales channel, by sales rep, and by customer. Most entrepreneurs neglect this task and it is not that hard. For products that are consistently low margin, find out why. Maybe you can raise prices, figure out how to make the product cheaper, or drop the product. If you cannot make a decent living with the product, why keep making it? If a particular sales channel is low margin, dig deeper to determine why. Maybe the sales staff needs more training or maybe you need a different channel. If you have a customer with existing pricing that does not allow you to make money, I suggest you raise prices. If the customer won't accept the price increase, fire the customer.

When preparing price quotes or bids, try to push the margin by a small amount. For example if your normal markup allows for an 18% gross profit, try pushing it to 18.5%. Guess what happens? Typically, you make more money. The price increase is so minor that most customers won't notice it. Entrepreneurs often get into habits of pricing a product or service in certain way or at a historical markup. After a while, we don't think about it anymore. Instead, we just do it.

If you are pricing on value and the customer needs a product or service in a hurry, charge them a premium. Rush charges or overtime charges are a common practice in most industries. Bill them accordingly. You came through for the customer and you deserve a reward. Generally, they are more than willing to pay for getting the goods on time.

Sell and promote your high-margin products. If you make more money on a particular product or product line, use your promotion dollars to push those products. Not long ago, a consulting client who ran a chain of pizza kitchens needed some help with product promotion. As with most pizza shops, pizza got the customer in the store, but it was the lowest margin product on the menu. Meanwhile, the margin on pasta was multiples better. My consulting team challenged the owner to focus all his in-store promotion on pasta instead of pizza. We recommended that he have the waiters push pasta specials, that the menu be focused on pasta with pizza on the back of the menu. The daily special display board listed only pasta. In addition, that we created contests for employees to sell more pasta, created kids' pasta menu items, and promoted dinner combos of pizza and pasta. Guess what? He sold more pasta and made more money.

You can also make more profit by selling more goods and services to your most profitable customers; you can do this simply by tracking their sales more closely. I suggest that you set up a detailed tracking system to monitor their purchasing behavior. Let's say that you track their purchases for a twelve-week period. When you anticipate a shortage or a dip in your product's inventory at the customer site, call them before they call you. Surprise them with your knowledge of their business and get them to order the replacement product now. If it is a commodity product, this tactic might increase your market share and it will demonstrate that you care about their business.

Review your suppliers' pricing. Like your own price and margin decisions, it is easy to fall in the habit of buying the same supplies at the same prices from the same supplier. Consider renegotiating better pricing from your existing suppliers. It is amazing what happens when just ask a supplier for a lower price; often they will lower it on the spot. Consider new suppliers; increased margins might just be phone call away. Offer to buy in bulk if you can get a pricing reduction. You could also offer to pay net 15 in exchange for a lower price.

Take a shot at this: Try adjusting your gross profit upward by .5%; see if anyone even notices or remarks about it during the next 60 days. If not, do it again next month. You may have priced your product too low.

97. Customer Testimonials Help You Sell

"I can live for two months on a good compliment."

Mark Twain (1835–1910) Author and humorist

The best salesperson for an entrepreneurial venture is a happy customer. A prospective customer often will struggle with the idea of buying a product or a solution from a new vendor or a start up venture. To be blunt, they don't trust you and they don't believe most of what you tell them. Yet, if they can read or listen to a testimonial from one of your happy customers, it can make the decision to buy from you much easier.

A testimonial is a written or recorded endorsement from a customer, which describes their happiness with your product or solution; consider these kind words as evidence or proof that what you say about your firm or product is true. The first requirement in getting a testimonial is making a customer happy; you earn testimonials by doing things right. Next, you need them to put their testimonial in writing to you. Some happy customers will send a thank you letter on their own accord, but most won't. When a customer says "thank you" or "good job," ask them to write it down. Typically, they will do so cheerfully. I recommend that you keep a file of these positive remarks and look at them periodically; at the very least, they will cheer you up. With their permission, you can include their testimonials on your website, in e-mail campaigns, or in your brochure material.

Good testimonials are written by real people and sound that way. Be careful to not edit them or sanitize them, since you could lose the intent or feel of the original author. The testimonial should focus on one event; don't cloud the success with too many facts or parameters. The published testimonial should include the customer's name, the firm name, and location. The best testimonials refer to some metric or measurement of success such as "the use of this product decreased my through-put time by 10%".

Always be on the hunt for testimonials. Routine customer service follow-up calls present a perfect opportunity to get this good news in writing. Remember to get the kind words in writing, but you also need to be specific about how you intend to use the testimonial. You may find some large companies may have restrictions on their buyers, which precludes this practice.

Video testimonials can now be done easily and cheaply; they can be powerful tools to overcome objections such as pricing or single sourcing. For the prospect that won't give you an appointment, a video testimonial DVD mailed to the client might open the door. I recommend that every website have a tab called "testimonials", or better yet, call it "happy customers." This tab could house written testimonials and video testimonials.

If you are using a testimonial in your sales letter or brochure copy, be sure to place the testimonial quote near the feature or benefit it describes. Testimonials may be the best way to convince a prospect to buy now.

Take a risk: Ask your favorite customer if they will do a video testimonial. The worst thing that can happen is that they will say no; but they will be very flattered, since you asked them. More than likely, they will say yes.

98. *Loyal Customers Keep on Coming Back*

"The best way to keep loyalty in a man's heart is to keep money in his purse."

Irish Proverb

Loyal customers keep on coming back. Loyalty is earned after the sale has been made and after the product or solution has been delivered. It is all about their perception of value. This perception is the reward that you get for delivering what you promised in quality, service, and responsiveness. More than just satisfied, a loyal customer refers you to other potential customers. They value the relationship with you and they want your business to succeed. These customers are worth their weight in gold.

A loyal customer often pays more and they won't stop to haggle when placing an order. They are confident in your product or solution and they feel that you need to be fairly compensated. Since you know them and their special needs, servicing this customer is easy. The sheer repetition helps. When there is a problem, they know by experience that you will make things right. They have a great dialog with you, so they offer suggestions on how you might improve the product. They help you design the next generation of product.

For many businesses, the repeat customer is the lifeblood of the business. Invest in your repeat customers as much as you invest in your new business development efforts. Frankly, you want to keep these folks coming back, so consider the creation of a customer loyalty program.

There are a few common types of loyalty programs. A rewards program entitles frequent customers to earn perks or rewards based on sales volume. The gifts could range from simple gratuities to vacations depending on the size of the business and the "gifting" practices in your industry. Entertainment gifts may be the most common reward such as tickets to sporting events or the theater. A membership program can provide incentives such as discounts, freebies, free shipping, and other earned incentives. The member carries a special card and gets special access to sales events. There is a practice in the haberdashery business called "trunk sales" or "invitation-only sales". A clothing store will hold a private sale for loyal customers; in this case, the customer gets a first look at new merchandise along with special pricing.

Once you have identified a customer as loyal, make sure they stay that way. Stay in touch with them. Send note cards saying thanks. Keep them updated by e-mail. Visit them. Have lunch or coffee with them. Remember significant dates such as birthdays, graduation days, or anniversaries. Holiday cards are great, but they all come at once. Consider Thanksgiving cards as novel way to stay in touch; they are seldom given but they are remembered. If a client has been sick or was injured, follow up with them. Let them know that you care. Say thanks again and again.

Tip: Send a note card to your best customers thanking them for their business.

99. Be the Firm That is Easy to Do Business With

"Before enlightenment, chop wood, carry water. After enlightenment, chop wood, carry water."

Zen Buddhist Proverb

I was in Kiev, Ukraine a few years back and was invited by some Ukrainian friends to lunch; they wanted me to try some "real Ukrainian" food. They knew just where to go, or so they thought. We walked up to the front door of their "favorite restaurant" to discover a sign that ironically said, "Closed for lunch, come back later". My friends, now rather embarrassed, took me to another restaurant that was "just as good". All through lunch, I kept on thinking about the other restaurant and how important it is for a business to be convenient, friendly, and available for the customer. "Being easy to work with" is achieved by focusing your perspective on the customer experience rather than your own. To be known as the firm that is "easy to do business with" a business needs to be different in some not-so-subtle ways:

- You need to be open 24 hours day, 7 days a week. Impossible you say? Not if you have a website which allows your customer to order online or leave a "contact us" message. You need to be open for business anytime the customer wants to buy. Remember, it is not your website; it is the customers' website.
- Use 800 numbers to send a message to the customer that you are available and convenient. They are relatively inexpensive and add a special touch. The 800 numbers say, "Please call me anytime." Remember to monitor the incoming calls or message mailbox routinely; a promptly returned phone call is always best.
- When an employee answers the phone, make sure that the employee "owns the phone call"; this policy ensures that the customer's question or issue doesn't get handed off or forgotten.
- Automated phone systems are great for saving money, but they can be lousy for the customer. Make sure that getting to a real person is easy to do. Nothing is more frustrating than getting lost in a complex automated phone system. Just as important, make sure that the voice that customer finally gets is friendly, informative, and understanding.

- Make it easy for the customer to complain. Customer complaints are golden opportunities to improve your product quality while securing a long-term relationship. When someone calls to complain, it is best to calmly listen, take careful notes, and commit to getting back with a plan or a solution. Follow through and fix the problem. Thank them for complaining. See the chapter called "The Rebound Effect: Effective Handling of Customer Complaints."
- Orders received need to be accepted, processed, and confirmed promptly. No exceptions. Invoices need to error free and delivered on time. Include customer purchase order numbers and reference numbers, not just your invoice numbers. This practice can help you get paid sooner.
- Flexible payment terms can make a huge difference in a customer's perception of your firm. Offering net 60 instead of net 30 could make doing business easy today. Your flexibility will be remembered.
- Offer a "guarantee" to minimize customer fears; although most customers will never exercise it, it will make them feel better about doing business with your firm.
- Make sure that your website is easy to use by being up to date and well designed; make sure that all your links are "live" and function properly.
- Finally, ask your customers frequently for suggestions on how to make doing business with your firm easier. Survey their satisfaction continuously. Then, do what they suggest.

Final tip: When a customer needs something or has a special request, use the words "Consider it done" or "It will be my pleasure". These very simple words are very powerful. They will reassure the buyer.

100. Do Business by Accident at Trade Shows

"Never be the first to arrive at a party or the last to go home,
and never, ever be both."

David Brown (1959–2003) Astronaut

Trade shows can be very high impact events, if you plan ahead.

First, make sure that the event draws your target market. Consider attending the trade show first as a visitor so you can scope it out. This may not always be practical and trade shows can change from year to year. However, it is probably a safe bet that if your customers went last year, they will go again.

Doing business by accident means working the booths and crowd. Be sure to wear a nametag that clearly identifies who you are and what you do. People may be looking for you, so make it easy for them to find you. If attending and not exhibiting, let your customers know ahead of time and set up appointments at the show. It makes for a great "meet and greet" environment.

As an exhibitor, you need to prepare in advance. Contact the firm coordinating the event to determine table or booth size. Some events have very specific rules while others will let you customize your space. Drawing attention to your booth can be done with bright colors on a backdrop, a tablecloth, or signage. Demonstrations are very appropriate at this type of event; have a PowerPoint or video continuously playing your product's pitch. Brochures should be made available to handle any size of crowd; it is a marketing disaster to run out of brochure material, samples, or business cards at these events. Sadly, this happens all the time when you don't plan for success.

This is definitely the time for a "tchotchke" (Yiddish for gift or goodie). The options are endless, but think evergreen. You want the visitor at your booth to take something away with them that will live on their desk forever; it must have your company name, logo, and contact information. Common examples are coffee cups, pens, paperweights, and mouse pads. Get creative. People love gifts and they will go out of their way to visit your booth for the right tchotchke. A local real estate agent gave my favorite tchotchke of all time to me; it was a half-pound container of salt! The container had the real estate agent's smiling face and contact information on the label; it still sits in my kitchen pantry. Since I don't use much salt, I imagine that I will be looking at that real estate agent's face for about the next decade or so.

Consider having a drawing for a prize such as an iPod or a Blackberry. To enter the drawing, your visitor must drop off a business card in a fishbowl at your booth or they must let you scan their conference ID badge. Follow up with everyone and let them know what happened. Get them in your prospect database.

To draw people to your booth, appeal to their senses. Pleasant smells work like cinnamon, cookies, or flowers. Nothing beats good eye contact or smiling faces. Balloons get attention. It is a bit sexist, but pretty women or handsome men will attract visitors to the booth. Soft music can make you different, depending on the image you want to promote. You can piggyback on a popular theme such as a movie; dress everyone up like the movie characters. Remember if your customer does not come to the booth, you have achieved nothing.

Try this: Ask your current customers what trade shows they regularly attend. You might consider attending them as a visitor if they are new to you. Your new prospects could be there waiting for you.

101. Guarantees Minimize Customer Fear

"Promise only what you can deliver. Then deliver more
than you promise."

Unknown

Many customers hesitate to buy because they fear that they might make the wrong decision and regret it later. This fear dominates the purchase decision and may kill the selling opportunity altogether. One way to minimize this fear, or even eliminate it altogether, is to offer a guarantee.

This is not as crazy as it sounds. Presuming your product or service is good and you have few complaints, a guarantee might help you sell more. We know that most customers don't bother to complain, even when they are unhappy. In fact, most unhappy customers just go away and never tell you why. Maybe the guarantee will help them express their displeasure or pain; this will allow you the chance to save the customer relationship. For the prospective customer, maybe the guarantee will help minimize the risk of doing business with your firm.

Here is the trick: you probably already have an implicit guarantee. For example, if a customer calls you with a quality problem, don't you fix it or replace the defective product? Don't you normally bend over backwards when the unhappy customer calls? Of course you do, because it just makes good sense to do so. The point is that most of us already have a guarantee policy and just don't put it on our website or our purchase agreements. Think how powerful it is tell a prospective client that you guarantee your work, your product, or your service.

I recommend specific guarantees that describe what is important to your customer. If you are in a niche service business, you already know what that core deliverable is and can consistently deliver it. If that is the case, then guarantee it. FedEx knows that it can deliver overnight anywhere by 10:30 a.m. the next day with a 99% success rate. They believe so strongly in this commitment and in their abilities that they offer a service guarantee. FedEx customers know that they can depend on their valuable packages arriving on time. A specific guarantee lets the prospective customer know that they need not worry.

Some consumer product based businesses offer guarantees that are "money back" regardless of the customer issue. This type of guarantee is a branding feature, which helps differentiate the business from the competition. I have found "money back" guarantees to be most successful when used for low-priced consumer products and services. Recently, I have seen some guarantees that offer 110% or greater money back, which is going overboard from my perspective. It just begs for manipulation from the lunatic fringe of your customer base.

There also seems less cachet and greater financial risk for money back guarantees when selling industrial products or high priced goods. For example, you don't see money back guarantees on Honda automobiles. Satisfaction guarantees are often a better alternative for these products; promise to make things right, but you don't give away the farm in the process.

Also, don't confuse a guarantee with a mere cancellation for convenience. I have seen guarantees backfire when a customer is given unconditional cancellation privileges. This can be particularly injurious to long-term service contracts, when the full contract period is needed to ensure sufficient margin.

Finally, like most new ideas, you should test this guarantee first. Try out the guarantee on a customer or customer group. See what happens. With a successful trial, a customer-wide rollout will go more smoothly. Make this guarantee a key feature of your sales presentations, a tab on your website, a benefit on your brochures, and a part of your mission statement.

Put a toe in the water: Next time you sell something, tell the customer that they can call you for any reason. If they are ever dissatisfied, tell them that you will make it better or give them their money back. Give them your business card with your direct line handwritten on the back.

102. Don't Fight the Marketplace

"Change before you have to."

Jack Welch (1935–) Businessman

A wise friend of mine told me once that all good things last two years. It sounds a bit cynical, but I think what he meant was that there is a life cycle to all things including products, jobs, companies, and ideas. Implied in his message was to not rest on your laurels or revel in your past glories too long, since change may be just around the corner.

This same thinking applies to marketing in an entrepreneurial setting. Things can change quickly, which can dramatically change the needs of your target customer and thus challenge you to quickly change your product or solution. My experience is that these changes generally come with warning signs or cues, which will allow you time to adjust. Your intimacy with your niche will provide you a competitive advantage, but it will be up to you to positively greet the changes rather than sticking to your existing methods or designs.

A good example of a major shift in a market is the advent of digital music downloads with MP3 formats. For decades, the music industry has fought tooth and nail to protect their intellectual property on vinyl records, then on tapes, then on CDs, and now on the iPod. Over the last five years, the music industry has been forced to change their entire business model to accommodate the changing needs of their customer. In this case, technology was the driver of the change with the new affordable MP3 format, which allowed digital music to be downloaded legally, or otherwise, to a low-cost portable MP3 player. The technology allowed customers to get exactly what they wanted, which was the ability to listen to the individual songs from their own customized, portable music players.

While the court battles raged between the giant music companies and the technology makers, the customer voted their preference for the MP3 format. Case closed. For some in the music business, this has allowed new packaging and marketing opportunities. Apple created iTunes and the customer got what they wanted. The lesson is simple. Don't fight battles that cannot be won. Instead, use the market shifts to your advantage and be a player in the new game.

Ponder this: Is there any major change on the horizon for your business or for your customer? Are you embracing it, ignoring it, or fighting it?

103. A Business School Tool That Helps Solve Marketing Problems

"Whenever you see a successful business, someone once made a courageous decision."

Peter Drucker (1909–2006) Author and professor

When confronted with a difficult or complex marketing decision, it helps to slow down and analyze the situation. For example, you might need to make a decision about the entry into a new market that seems to fit your product, but has unique selling challenges. A business school tool that helps with this type of problem solving is called a "SWOT analysis": Strengths, Weaknesses, Opportunities, and Threats. This simple tool helps you organize your thinking by challenging you to look at an opportunity or problem from four different perspectives. A SWOT analysis helps you from overlooking key issues by focusing too much on one aspect of the situation.

A SWOT analysis helps you summarize your analysis, your research or findings. You can use a SWOT analysis to analyze your firm, a product, a campaign, or most anything.

There are four parts in a SWOT analysis:

Strengths are internal characteristics at your firm that will positively impact the future for your firm or product. Simply stated, these strengths should be significant factors that will support the proposed idea or objective. These strengths must be sustainable for the long term and not just serendipity. An example of "strength" would be an intimate knowledge of the customer needs and wants because of your long-term association with the industry.

Weaknesses are internal factors at your firm that may be negative or might negatively impact the support of the proposed idea or objective. These weaknesses will or could derail the progress or success of an objective. An example of this would be a lack of adequate capital to finance a new venture.

Opportunities are factors in the external environment that your firm (and others) may be able to take advantage of or exploit. Typically, an opportunity is not unique to just your firm, but is also available to others with similar skills or ambitions. An opportunity is something that your firm or your competitor can utilize to meet the objective. An example of this would be a change in government regulation or policy that allows customers new tax advantages by using your product.

Threats are aspects of the external environment that could derail or negatively impact the future for your firm (and others). An example of a threat would be the possible or probable introduction of a new technology that will make your solution and your competitors' solutions obsolete or less attractive. A threat is out of your control but a reality nonetheless.

Here is an example of a SWOT analysis for the current situation for Apple Computer. They seem to be on the top of the world with the unprecedented sales of the iPod and the increased market acceptance of their user-friendly computers. The marketplace has rewarded Apple with increased sales and profits and Apple is quite proud of its "reborn" market acceptance. The Apple stores have been a smash hit with consumers. Industry insiders suggest that innovation has become harder as the firm has increased its size. The past arrogance of senior management seems to have returned; it seems that Apple management is once again drunk on their success.

Meanwhile, the iPod's success has encouraged major investments by the competition, both domestic and offshore. The Chinese manufacturers have made great strides in manufacturing and innovation. The market for portable consumer electronics now includes five-year-olds who happily chat away on their cells phones, take digital photos, and listen to their MP3s. Consumers have increasingly less brand loyalty. Apple has chosen not embrace cellular technology (at least not at the time when this book was written). Some say that all digitized information will flow through the cell phone or even the watch. (Dick Tracy was just ahead of his time.) Applications for portable electronics include medical records, distance learning, and entertainment. What is next?

For you visual thinkers out there, here is how you can display the analysis in the four major buckets to help you organize your thinking. Below is a simple matrix that captures the relevant information and analysis:

Apple SWOT Analysis:

Strengths

1. A strong brand known for innovation and user friendly products.
2. A growing and successful retail channel.
3. Incredible market acceptance of the iPod with an upswing in Apple computers.

Opportunities

1. The use of portable and cellular electronics is reaching down to the five- year-olds.
2. Everything is getting digitized including music, information, medical records, etc.
3. Mobility and convenience are creating the need for more wireless and portable devices.

Weaknesses

1. Outright arrogance of senior management (i.e., Apple knows best).
2. Innovation has become harder as the firm becomes larger.
3. Lack of cellular technology.

Threats

1. Offshore competition is becoming more sophisticated and better at marketing.
2. Barriers to entry for the MP3 and other portable products are getting lower.
3. Decreasing brand loyalty of the consumer.
4. Advancements in wireless technology.

The above SWOT suggests that increased competition and a changing marketplace threaten Apple's current success. Their competitive advantage with iPod may not be sustainable. Clearly, they need to look forward to more portable cellular products to stay ahead of the curve. Other strategic questions spew from this analysis. Jack Welch says, "Change before you have to." Apple had better listen to Jack. Although a SWOT analysis won't make the hard decisions for you, it can organize your thinking.

Update: It looks like Apple just did a SWOT analysis. They just introduced the new Apple iPhone.

104. The Marketing Plan is Where Everything Comes Together

"Things are only impossible until they're not."

Jean-Luc Picard (1987–1994)
STAR TREK: THE NEXT GENERATION

Every firm, large or small, needs a marketing plan. A marketing plan is a subset of the company business plan; you will often hear people using the terms synonymously, but in error. While the business plan reviews all aspects of the organization, the marketing plan specifically reviews core issues of strategy, products, sales, promotion, and advertising. While there are many uses for a marketing plan, the primary uses are to secure financing, to set strategy on annual basis, to react to a change in the marketplace, or to address a new product opportunity.

When a firm seeks financing from a bank or outside source, a business plan is a basic requirement with the marketing plan as a typical focal point. Most investors will quickly turn to the pages devoted to marketing; the underlying question for the investor is what is different or better about this investment opportunity?

An intelligently managed enterprise will perform a full review of the marketing plan annually while monitoring progress on a monthly basis. Changes in the marketplace can cause the business to review its current plan. For example, a change in pricing at a significant competitor can trigger a review of the current plan and an adjustment to the current strategy.

Small changes in the external environment can challenge the entrepreneur to make wholesale changes to existing plans. In fact, nimble and quick reflexes may be one of the factors that favor the survival of small firms; although financial and analytical resources may be few, process and product changes come easier for the small firm compared to larger well-financed competitors who cannot move as quickly.

Finally, new opportunities can challenge the business to review and adjust marketing plans. An example would be a breakthrough technology in materials quality that now allows the manufacturer to make products to meet military specifications, which is a market the firm has never served.

The marketing plan comes in many shapes and sizes. I recommend that you have the following basic components:

Executive Summary

- One page that summarizes the plan for those with short attention spans (i.e., most investors)

Mission, Vision, Purpose

- Why does the business exist, what really matters, and where is the firm going?

Current Analysis

- Target Market and Industry Analysis—What does the external environment look like for the customer and the industry?
- Product or Service Description—An analysis of the unique features and benefits.
- Channel of Distribution—How is business conducted today?
- Competitive Analysis—What is the competition doing and how are they different?

Strategy, Goals, and Objectives

- Marketing Strategy—How is the firm going to position itself? What is the target market?
- Competitive Advantage—How will your solution be different or what will be done differently?
- Goals and Objectives—What does the firm aspire to do and how will it measure progress?

Marketing Mix Factors

- Customers Wants and Needs—Who is the target customer and what unique needs are there?
- Products or Services—What will you deliver and how does this match with the customers' needs?
- Promotion—How will your products get noticed in the marketplace?
- Pricing—What is your pricing strategy?
- Public Relations—What is your message? How will you generate publicity?

- Advertising—What is your plan to maximize the awareness of your product or service?
- Sales Methods—How will you sell your products or services?

Planning

- Forecasts—A monthly summary of sales goals for a five-year period.
- Budgets—Marketing expenses, cost of sales, cost of compensation, etc.
- Timeline—What is the plan for strategic and tactical activities?
- Measurement—What methods will be used to track and measure these factors and activities?

Summary

- One page that restates the obvious.

A final thought: Always seek third party feedback on your marketing plan; consider the help from one your personal board of directors. Get constructive criticism before you put the marketing plan in front of an investor or a potential partner.

105. I Don't Have Time to Implement All These Marketing Ideas

"It's better to feed one cat than many mice."

Old Norwegian Proverb

Entrepreneurs struggle to do it all. Whether it is closing one more sale, handling a personnel matter at the shop, or trying to collect aging invoices, there is never enough time to do it all. Call it a time management problem, a desire to do the very best work possible, or an obsessive-compulsive disorder; most entrepreneurs try to do too much. This means a lot of things don't get done on time or at all, and this includes marketing.

I am sure that you read all the books that recommend setting priorities, scheduling your time, and saying no to the other things that come along. That topic belongs in another book. For now, here are some ideas on how to get the marketing ideas implemented:

- Hire stay-at-home moms. Moms with kids at home often are highly educated and want to stay current in the job market, but can only work part-time. They need a break from the kids and will be grateful for the chance to contribute. Stay-at-home moms can be awesome workers and, since they are part-time, they are cheap.
- Hire college interns. Starving students at the local university are desperate for work experience and will do it free in exchange for a recommendation and the chance to put some real experience on their resumes. Contact the local university business department to discuss their intern program. The students will do great work and you might find future employees.
- Hire retired workers. Odds are they are wiser than you, will work harder than you, and won't complain about the coffee. Seriously, they may be best employees out there. Highly skilled and available for part-time work, they may be just what the doctor ordered.
- Consider getting help from SCORE (Service Corps of Retired Executives). SCORE is the "counselor to America's small businesses" and has helped 7.2 million small businesses. Their support is "free and confidential" (yes, you read that right); they have over 10,000 volunteers with over 600 business skills; most

are working or retired business owners, executives, and corporate leaders. I love these guys.

- Delegate marketing activities to your current staff. You are not a super-hero and you may be surprised how others on your team will "step up" to a new interesting task. You may be surprised that they can do the work as well as you or even better. Take a chance on them.

- Hire a consultant to do the work. Most consultants move from project to project, but would love the chance to go on a retainer with a client. The steady income and comfort of not having to remarket their services makes a retainer very attractive. For the contracting firm, you get access to skills unavailable at your firm and you get the work done.

Tip: Take Fridays off. Let the staff run the business on Friday, while you devote the day to attending to your marketing strategy at home or away from the office. Turn off the cell phone and concentrate on marketing one day a week.

106. Niche Markets Are Out There Waiting for You to Find Them

"We must be willing to get rid of the life we've planned, so as to have the life that is waiting for us."

Joseph Campbell (1904–1987) U.S. folklorist

The media spends most of its time telling us about the next big thing, while overlooking the power and the size of niche markets. For example, when the media speaks to us about retail, they tell us about the retail juggernaut Wal-Mart and not about the innovative niche marketers on eBay who serve unique buyers with special needs. The funny thing is that these eBay competitors collectively dwarf Wal-Mart.

Chris Anderson's book, THE LONG TAIL, cites the example of Wal-Mart's music selection of 4,500 titles; those titles have to sell to be carried as in-store inventory at Wal-Mart. If a title doesn't sell it is quickly removed from the shelves. End of story. Meanwhile, Amazon.com, which Anderson calls a "long tail aggregator", happily carries 800,000 titles since it has no worries about the costs of managing retail shelf space. In an exaggerated sense, Amazon is a giant niche provider, which serves hundreds, or maybe thousands of specialized niche music segments. His book suggests that it is harder and harder to be a Wal-Mart and that the marketplace is rapidly fragmenting into a highly diverse universe of unique niche markets that can now be easily served by internet-centric providers. The next big thing is actually going to be many new little things.

I have personally witnessed a similar metamorphosis in how I watch television. Maybe you have too. When I was kid living on the Kansas prairie, we had two television stations: CBS and NBC. I watched the same television shows that my friends did at the same time on the same night every week. For instance, the popular western TV series "Bonanza" was on Sunday nights at 9 p.m. My family watched this show, along with the mandatory commercial advertisements, as did most of my friends and their families. Flash forward to today and I have satellite TV with hundreds of stations along with TiVo. I have no idea what shows are on the networks and I have not watched a commercial in months. I watch only what I want when I want to watch it.

Our marketplace is being "personalized" with people buying goods ands services as individuals, not as crowds. This personalization of the overall marketplace is creating huge opportunities for the niche marketer. The key is to identify the niche market and make the solution available to the buyer, while visualizing your customer as an individual buyer with unique needs. The more you can personalize your product and the accompanying purchase process, the more likely you will sell your products or services. The one-size-fits-all mindsets are quickly giving away to an internet bazaar of niche providers. This won't happen overnight, but I recommend that you embrace the change rather than fight it.

It has never been better to be an entrepreneur. Go find your niche.

A final word: Go to my website http://firstbestordifferent.com and check out my blog at http://firstbestordifferent.com/blog . Let me know what you think about niche marketing.

Thanks for reading my book.

All the best, JBJ.

Epilogue

"Teachers open the door. You enter by yourself"

Chinese Proverb

BIBLIOGRAPHY

Allen, Kathleen, LAUNCHING NEW VENTURES: AN ENTREPRE-NEURIAL APPROACH, Houghton Mifflin Company, New York, 2006.

Anderson, Chris, THE LONG TAIL: WHY THE FUTURE OF BUSINESS IS SELLING LESS OF MORE, Hyperion, New York, New York, 2006.

Burg, Bob, ENDLESS REFERRALS: NETWORKING YOUR EVERY-DAY CONTACTS INTO SALES, McGraw-Hill, New York, 1994.

Butler-Bowdon, Tom, FIFTY SELF-HELP CLASSICS: FIFTY INSPI-RATIONAL BOOKS TO TRANSFORM YOUR LIFE, Nicholas Brealey Publishing, Incorporated, Yarmouth, Maine, 2005.

Carson, David, Stanley Cromie, Pauric McGowan, and Jimmy Hill, MAR-KETING AND ENTREPRENEURSHIP IN SMES: AN INNOVA-TIVE APPROACH. Prentice Hall, Upper Saddle River, New Jersey, 1995.

Clifford, Jr., Donald K. and Richard E. Cavanaugh, THE WINNING PER-FORMANCE, Bantam Dell Publishing Group, Westminster, Mary-land, 1991.

Covey, Stephen R., THE SEVEN HABITS OF HIGHLY EFFECTIVE PEOPLE, Simon & Schuster, Incorporated, New York, 1989.

Ferrazzi, Keith and Tahl Raz NEVER EAT ALONE: AND OTHER SECRETS TO SUCCESS, ONE RELATIONSHIP AT A TIME, Dou-ble Day, New York, 2005.

Fugere Brian, Chelsea Hardaway, and Jon Warshawsky WHY BUSINESS PEOPLE SPEAK LIKE IDIOTS: A BULLFIGHTER'S GUIDE, The Free Press, a division of Simon & Schuster, Incorporated, New York, 2005.

Gerber, Michael E., THE E-MYTH REVISITED: WHY MOST SMALL BUSINESSES DON'T WORK AND WHAT TO DO ABOUT IT, Harper Collins, New York, 2001.

Gladwell, Malcolm, THE TIPPING POINT: HOW LITTLE THINGS CAN MAKE A BIG DIFFERENCE, Little, Brown, and Company, New York, 2000.

Godin, Seth, ALL MARKETERS ARE LIARS: THE POWER OF TELLING AUTHENTIC STORIES IN A LOW-TRUST WORLD, Penguin Group, New York, 2005.

Godin, Seth, PERMISSION MARKETING: TURNING STRANGERS INTO FRIENDS AND FRIENDS INTO CUSTOMERS, Simon & Schuster, Incorporated, New York, 2001.

Gordan, Kim, MAXIMUM MARKETING MINIMUM DOLLARS, Kaplan Publishing, Chicago, 2006.

Helgesen, Sally, THRIVING IN 24/7: SIX STRATEGIES FOR TAMING THE NEW WORLD OF WORK, The Free Press, a division of Simon & Schuster, Incorporated, New York, 2001.

Hiam, Alexander and Charles D. Schewe, THE PORTABLE MBA IN MARKETING, John Wiley and Sons, New York, 1992.

Kaplan, Jack and Anthony C. Warren, PATTERNS OF ENTREPRENEURSHIP, John Wiley and Sons, New York, 2007.

Kawasaki, Guy, THE ART OF THE START: THE TIME-TESTED, BATTLE-HARDENED GUIDE FOR ANYONE STARTING ANYTHING, Penguin Books, London, 2004

Kotler, Philip and Gary Armstrong, PRINCIPLES OF MARKETING, Prentice Hall, Upper Saddle River, New Jersey, 2005.

Kotler, Philip and Kevin Lane Keller, MARKETING MANAGEMENT, Prentice Hall, Upper Saddle River, New Jersey, 1995.

Kragen, Ken, LIFE IS A CONTACT SPORT: TEN GREAT CAREER STRATEGIES THAT WORK, William Morrow and Company, Incorporated, New York, 1994.

Kuratko, Donald F. and Richard M. Hodgetts, ENTREPRENEURSHIP: THEORY, PROCESS, AND PRACTICE, Thomson South-Western, Mason, Ohio, 2007.

Levinson, Jay Conrad, GUERRILLA MARKETING FOR FREE: DOZENS OF NO-COST TACTICS TO PROMOTE YOUR BUSINESS AND ENERGIZE YOUR PROFITS, Houghton Mifflin Company, New York, 2003.

Lodish, Leonard M., Howard Morgan, and Amy Kallianpur, ENTREPRENEURIAL MARKETING: LESSONS FROM WHARTON'S PIONEERING MBA COURSE, John Wiley and Sons, New York, 2001.

MacPherson, Kim, PERMISSION-BASED E-MAIL MARKETING THAT WORKS!, Dearborn Trade, Chicago, 2001.

Morgen, Sharon Drew, SELLING WITH INTEGRITY: REINVENTING SALES THROUGH COLLABORATION, RESPECT, AND SERVING Berkeley Publishing Group, New York, 1997.

Porter, Michael, COMPETITIVE STRATEGY: TECHNIQUES FOR ANALYZING INDUSTRIES AND COMPETITORS, The Free Press, a division of Simon & Schuster, Incorporated, New York, 1980.

Rogers, Everett M., DIFFUSION OF INNOVATIONS, The Free Press, a division of Simon & Schuster, Incorporated, New York, 1995.

Seligman, Martin, LEARNED OPTIMISM: HOW TO CHANGE YOUR MIND AND YOUR LIFE, Vintage Books, London, 2005.

Sharp, David J., CASES IN BUSINESS ETHICS, Sage Publications, Incorporated, Thousand Oaks, California, 2006.

WIKIPEDIA: THE FREE ENCYCLOPEDIA
http://en.wikipedia.org

Index

Come Visit

www.firstbestordifferent .com

First, *Best*, or *Different*

What Every Entrepreneur Needs to Know About Niche Marketing

- Read John Bradley Jackson's blog and share ideas at http://firstbestordifferent.com/blog/.
- Sign up for the quarterly newsletter; it's free!
- Download free articles on niche marketing and negotiation; listen to audio clips by the author.
- Visit the "Resources Page" for great marketing tools; find referrals to other marketing professionals.
- Contact the author directly (remember, he always calls or writes back).
- Get your book signed by the author with a personal inscription; he will write almost anything you want!
- View other cool marketing products including webinars, website design, business plan software, and e-books.
- Read an excerpt from the new book "What Every Entrepreneur Needs to Know About Negotiation and Conflict" by John Bradley Jackson. Available in the summer of 2007.

Whatever you do, remember to be first, best, or different!

Printed in the United States
204164BV00006B/1-9/A